Education

Social Sciences

Natural Sciences

Humanities

The Environmental Crisis

Man's Struggle to Live with Himself

Based on a lecture series organized
by the Yale School of Forestry with
funds from The Ford Foundation

THE ENVIRONMENTAL CRISIS

MAN'S STRUGGLE TO LIVE WITH HIMSELF

edited by Harold W. Helfrich, Jr.

New Haven and London, Yale University Press

Copyright © 1970 by Yale University.
Third printing, July 1970.
All rights reserved. This book may not be
reproduced, in whole or in part, in any form
(except by reviewers for the public press),
without written permission from the publishers.
Library of Congress catalog card number: 79-105456
ISBN: 0-300-01312-4 (cloth), 0-300-01313-2 (paper)
Designed by Sally Sullivan,
set in IBM Selectric Press Roman type,
and printed in the United States of America by
The Carl Purington Rollins Printing-Office
of the Yale University Press.
Distributed in Great Britain, Europe,
and Africa by Yale University Press, Ltd.,
London; in Canada by McGill-Queen's University
Press, Montreal; in Mexico by Centro
Interamericano de Libros Académicos, Mexico
City; in Australasia by Australia and New
Zealand Book Co., Pty., Ltd., Artarmon, New
South Wales; in India by UBS Publishers'
Distributors Pvt., Ltd., Delhi; in Japan by
John Weatherhill, Inc., Tokyo.
"The Plight" from Design with Nature by Ian
McHarg. Copyright © by Ian McHarg. Reprinted
by permission of Doubleday & Company, Inc.

Contents

Foreword

It is a genuine pleasure for me to contribute a brief foreword for this book of lectures which comprised a 1968–69 symposium on "Issues in Environmental Crises" at the Yale University School of Forestry.

The symposium was conceived and programmed by F. Herbert Bormann, Oastler Professor of Forest Ecology, and Garth K. Voigt, Margaret K. Musser Professor of Forest Soils. Its success was so evident that it is being continued and expanded during the 1969–70 academic year; it is under the guidance of former U. S. Secretary of the Interior Stewart L. Udall, who is Visiting Professor (Adjunct) of Environmental Humanism at Yale and Chairman of the OVERVIEW Group, an international consulting firm on natural resources conservation.

These lecture series are made possible through a grant to the Yale School of Forestry from the Ford Foundation for a program in terrestrial ecology and ecosystem management. Their help and encouragement is hereby acknowledged with sincere gratitude.

Ever since primitive man first stalked warily out onto the grassy plains from the forested cradle of his species, he has been clawing his way toward civilization at the expense of his environment. His spectacular progress has brought him to the brink of destruction—possible in hours by nuclear conflict, and almost certainly in a few more centuries if he continues to multiply in numbers and befoul his planet Earth.

It is totally in character for the Yale School of Forestry to enter the battle against ignorance of the critically important ecological issues. The School was founded in response to a national need in 1900: the timber famine. During the intervening years, it has accomplished much to help solve that particular problem. Now it must provide leadership and imagination, and must train experts who will be able to cope with this new threat against all organisms.

On behalf of the Yale School of Forestry, I wish to proffer my thanks to Professors Bormann and Voigt for their immeasurable contributions toward the future achievement of these goals. My appreciation extends, too, to the distinguished authorities who served as lecturers and whose recorded wisdom has been preserved in this book.

François Mergen
Dean
School of Forestry
Yale University

INTRODUCTION

The sixth decade of the twentieth century finds mankind confronted by an unyielding paradox. Many people have concluded that because we are at the pinnacle of technological achievement, with an amazing list of accomplishments to our credit, our scientific ability to control and shape the human environment is without limit. Yet, even as our technical ability grows there is a steady and seemingly inexorable deterioration of our environment. The rising crescendo of discord created by unplanned and unforeseen technological by-products is beginning to penetrate the ears of even the most optimistic. Man's footprints are on the moon, but on earth hardly a stream remains free of pollution, palls of smog shroud our cities, pesticides telescope their deadly effects through worldwide food chains, beauty falls before the omnivorous advance of urban sprawl, and unrest and violence dominate our decaying cities and our illustrious universities.

Today's problems may be but the tip of an iceberg, that portion of a vast ecological catastrophe visible in the daily reporting of TV, radio, and newspaper. Beneath the surface, yet to be discovered by most of our citizens, lies the mass of a still more serious problem—the potential destruction of the balanced natural system that sustains life on this planet. This threat, in all its aspects, to the quality and even the very existence of life constitutes the environmental crisis—the central problem of modern man.

Our present dangerous position has not befallen us overnight. It has grown from two great forces that feed and reinforce each other: (1) unrestricted growth of man's numbers on a planet with finite capacity to provide for man's needs and absorb his garbage and (2) unrestricted technology coupled with an attitude of exploitative dominance of his environment. Our numbers have now reached the point where this attitude of dominance is no longer tolerable and we are being faced with the same physical limitations that regulate all biological populations. Unless population growth is checked there is no hope, even with our highly honed technological capabilities—capabilities which, unfortunately, are generally oriented toward exploitation rather than salvation.

Through this pervading gloom shines one ray of promise—the younger generation whose fumbling but perceptive rebellion is forcing reexamination of our philosophy toward natural and human resources. Together we are beginning to recognize that failure to appreciate the interrelatedness of the elements and all organisms or to calculate the real costs we must pay for alteration of our environment has led to a withering of the very amenities of a dignified life to which all are entitled and toward which our efforts are presumably directed.

What is the role of the university in this metamorphosis? It seems to us to be threefold: to instill new vigor into the ageless debate on the goals of society; to promote more studies and teaching on the interrelatedness of life rather than to build isolated specialties; and, finally, to help bridge the information gap between humanists concerned with the quality of life, environmental scientists, and those who manage our environment for human purposes.

It was in this spirit that we conceived the "Issues in the Environmental Crises" symposium. Our objective in this series was to analyze not only technological aspects but to probe moral, economic, and social facets as well. Our hope is to stimulate ideas and actions that may contribute to solutions.

F. H. Bormann
G. K. Voigt

Men's need for a better life has altered earth's balance and endangered its supply of natural resources by his own inventions —

Playing Russian Roulette with Biogeochemical Cycles

LaMont C. Cole

In view of the alterations man has made on the world environment, he has been extremely lucky to have stayed around for so long. We humans have presumed to adopt the label *Homo sapiens*, the wise one. We had better start living up to that label quickly if we are going to continue to survive here.

Ever since our Neolithic ancestors started using fire as a tool—probably first to drive game and later to clear forest land for grazing—man has been altering the face of every continent on which he has lived. It was sheer serendipity that these grasslands, created by burning forests, developed soils which eventually made them among the world's most valuable agricultural land. Our own prairies were probably created by fire, and maintained by fire and later by heavy grazing. Many other grasslands in other parts of the world fall into the same category. It is probable that in the continent of Africa, which has perhaps been inhabited by man since his origin, nothing of the landscape is as it would have been without him. The savannas were probably created and maintained by fire, and have become highly productive of a diverse fauna of grazing and browsing mammals. These mammals probably expanded from relative obscurity to tremendous numbers as a result of this alteration of their environment.

From the beginning, however, fire had some other less desirable effects. Smoke polluted the air, and the barren slopes of hills

LaMont C. Cole is professor of ecology at Cornell University. He is currently president of the American Institute of Biological Sciences. He is a former president of the Ecological Society of America, and former chairman of the Cornell Department of Zoology and of the Cornell Section of Ecology and Systematics. For many years he served as editor of Ecology magazine, and has often advised academic and governmental agencies on problems concerning environmental biology.

started to erode. The burned materials and erosion polluted streams and, on occasion, blocked them, producing swamps and marshes.

Later, man started his serious agricultural efforts on the flood plains of rivers where the land was fertile and well watered and easy to cultivate with simple tools. The valleys of such rivers as the Tigris, the Euphrates, the Nile, and the Indus thus became cradles of civilization. Human populations expanded and felt the need for more land and year-round cultivation. Then they built dams and canals for irrigation, often without providing adequate drainage; under such conditions water will move upward through the soil and evaporate at the surface, depositing a layer of salt there and so destroying fertility. Early men cut the forests from sloping land, causing flooding and erosion and filling of the irrigation works with silt. The grazing of their sheep and cattle accelerated the destruction of the land.

Destruction was so thorough that by the twelfth century Otto of Freising could write in his *Chronicon,* "But what now is Babylon—a shrine of sirens, a home of lizards and ostriches, a den of serpents."

By Otto's time pollution had also apparently come to Europe. He tells us that when Frederick Barbarossa's armies arrived in Rome in the summer of 1167, "The ponds, caverns, and ruinous places around the city were exhaling poisonous vapors and the air in the entire vicinity had become densely laden with pestilence and death." It must have been something like driving into New Haven from the airport.

It is difficult to say how much was known about water pollution in medieval times, but St. Hildegarde had an interesting comment on the Rhine in the thirteenth century. The river's name, incidentally, is supposedly derived from the German word for "clear." She wrote that its waters, if drunk unboiled, "would produce noxious blue fluids in the body."

Certainly, as civilization and urbanization progressed, pollution problems became more acute. By the year 1800, Samuel Taylor Coleridge could write:

"The river Rhine, it is well known,
Doth wash your city of Cologne:
But tell me, Nymphs, what power divine
Shall henceforth wash the river Rhine?"

In its early stages urbanization displayed unnoticed detrimental effects which we are barely beginning to appreciate today. Nature's way of dealing with refuse is to recycle it. Dead plant and animal matter breaks down and releases chemical nutrients which are quickly seized by other living organisms and re-used. But a city brings together subsistence materials originating over a wide area and concentrates them in a very small space. When it is time to dispose of the remnants, the materials cannot be recycled locally but must somehow be dispersed. Industry is now encouraging planned obsolescence which further accelerates the accumulation of waste. At the present time the refuse produced in this country is estimated to be increasing about 4 percent per year; this, by no coincidence, is about the same as the yearly increase in the Gross National Product.

The processes I have been discussing, chiefly burning and the acceleration of erosion and siltation, merely accentuate processes that could have gone on without man. A new dimension was added when man began exploitation of fossil fuels: peat, coal, natural gas, petroleum. It is recorded that in 1306 a citizen of London was tried and executed for burning coal in the city; three centuries later this was the way of life, and London had a smog problem. The profession of chimney sweeping was born and with it one of the earliest and the most striking examples of severe industrial pathology: cancer of the scrotum, induced by soot. (I was fascinated to learn recently that Los Angeles has a new law banning the burning of coal in the city. So we appear to have gone full circle.)

Even much earlier, small-scale examples of specific industrial contamination had occurred without appreciation of their significance. The Romans mined lead in Britain and smelted it there. It is said that the sites of those ancient smelting operations can still be recognized from the impoverished vegetation growing on the poisoned soil. However, not until the Industrial Revolution was in full swing could anyone have seen the full portent of such developments.

So man gradually shifted to a way of life based on the exploitation of fossil fuel. Through most of the period coal was the important source of energy, and not until this century was its supremacy challenged by petroleum. Populations multiplied, cities grew, and industry expanded explosively. Now, really just in the period since World War II, we have encountered an entirely new dimension of environmental deterioration. We have become so dependent on fossil fuels that surveys have found farmers expending more calories to run their machinery than they remove from their land in crops. Industrial plants, transportation—especially by automobile—and the heating requirements of an expanding world population have brought the combustion of fossil fuels to the point where we are actually causing measurable changes in the composition of the earth's atmosphere. As we shall see, we are risking much more serious changes in the atmosphere than anything else noted so far.

Never before has man been able to spread a particular pollutant over the entire surface of the earth. DDT is a case in point. It has been recovered from the fat of Antarctic seals and penguins, from fish all over the high seas, and from the ice of Alaskan glaciers. We have been incredibly lucky that DDT has not turned out to be a more noxious pollutant than it is. If it had possessed certain properties that no one had known about until it was too late, it could have brought an end to life on earth. If you are comforted by the thought that DDT is apparently not so bad as it might have been, reflect on this fact: the U.S. Food and Drug Administration estimates that we are now exposing ourselves and our environment to over a half million different chemicals, all of which must eventually be imposed on the earth environment. And this number is estimated to be increasing by 400 to 500 new chemicals per year.

Can our run of luck continue? Consider what new types of things we have asked the environment to assimilate just since

World War II: synthetic pesticides, plastics, antibiotics, radioisotopes, detergents.

The detergents make an interesting case. A few years ago on Long Island and elsewhere, people got excited about detergents because suds were coming out of their faucets. They demanded that something be done about it, and the chemical manufacturers came up with so-called biodegradable detergents. People no longer see the detergents, and now they think the problem has been solved. Actually, these biodegradable detergents are more toxic to many forms of aquatic life than the old detergents were, and they are also phosphorus compounds. So, while there is a worldwide shortage of phosphorus, we are throwing it away at such a rate that it has become one of our most significant water pollutants!

Another interesting case involving detergents concerns the tanker *Torrey Canyon* which was wrecked off the south coast of Great Britain and dumped a tremendous amount of petroleum onto the ocean. The Royal Navy and Royal Air Force went to work spraying the area with detergent. Fortunately, the Plymouth Laboratory of the Marine Biological Association of the United Kingdom turned over its entire facilities to study the effects of the spraying on marine life. They found some very interesting things. Where petroleum—untouched by the detergent—was washed up on rocky shores, the marine snails went around cleaning up the shore. The snails could eat the oil-soaked vegetation and suffer no harm from it. But where the detergents formed an emulsion with the oil, the snails were killed, and the mess was worse than if they had not used the detergents.

We are at most a few generations away from running out of the fossil fuels on which our economy, including agriculture, now depends. Current thinking holds that our next source of energy will be nuclear fuel.

This raises some very disturbing thoughts. Before scientists learned to control the release of atomic energy, the entire amount of radioactivity under man's mastery consisted of about 10 grams of radium—10 curies of radioactivity scattered among the world's hospitals. Today, a nuclear power plant is being built on the shores of Lake Ontario a few miles from Oswego, New York, that is going to put 130 curies per day into the atmosphere. This is a prodigious quantity of radioactivity, and it will be from a not particularly large reactor. Knowing that exposure to radioactivity shortens life, causes malignancies, and can produce genetic effects that can damage future generations, have we any cause for complacency?

If it turns out that we cannot run our economy on nuclear energy, that we cannot live with the atom and survive, then our remaining hope for a big source of energy is sunlight. This is a very diffuse form of energy, and the problems of concentrating it into usable form will be tremendous.

Past civilizations trusted to luck and disappeared. Modern Iraq could not produce food for anything like the population of the once-great Babylonian Empire; nor could Iran (except for the income from oil) support the Persian civilization of Darius I; nor could modern Guatemala or Yucatan support the Mayan civilization.

Few laymen realize that our atmosphere as we know it today is a biological product, that it has probably remained essentially unchanged in composition for at least 300 million years up to this present century. By volume the atmosphere at sea level, neglecting contaminants, consists of about 78 percent nitrogen, about 21 percent oxygen, 0.03 percent carbon dioxide, and traces of other gases. Nitrogen is actually a scarce element on earth; 99.9 percent of the mass of all known terrestrial matter consists of 18 elements—and nitrogen is not among the 18. So what is so much nitrogen doing in the atmosphere? Oxygen is the most abundant of all the chemical elements, but it is a highly reactive chemical which outside of the atmosphere is almost never found in uncombined form. So what is so much free oxygen doing in the atmosphere?

The answers to both questions are biological. Certain bacteria and algae take nitrogen from the atmosphere and convert it into ammonia, which is a toxic material. If the story stopped at this stage, we should all be poisoned when we breathed.

Two additional types of microorganisms in the soil and water are responsible for converting the ammonia to nitrate. Green plants absorb the nitrate and ammonia and use the nitrogen in building plant proteins. Then microorganisms and animals get the nitrogen for their proteins directly or indirectly from the proteins of plants. When plants and animals die, decomposer organisms—again primarily microorganisms—break down the proteins, mostly to ammonia; and this little cycle, ammonia to nitrate, nitrate to protein, protein to ammonia can repeat.

If the story stopped at this stage, the atmosphere would long ago have run out of nitrogen. Fortunately, there are still additional types of microorganisms that can convert nitrate to molecular nitrogen and so maintain the composition of the atmosphere.

Twice I have heard sophisticated chemists say—and once I read this in a high-school biology textbook—that it would be desirable to block the activities of these so-called denitrifying bacteria. It impressed them as a dirty trick that when some organisms go to all the trouble of giving fixed nitrogen to the soil, others would come along and release it. They did not recognize that what they were proposing, if it could be done successfully, would bring an end to life on earth. So we see that quite a variety of microorganisms involved in the nitrogen cycle are essential for the continuation of life.

But what thought does industrialized man give to the welfare of these forms? With reckless abandon he dumps his half million chemical forms into soil, water, and air, not knowing whether one of these chemicals, or some combination of them, might be a deadly poison for one of the steps in the nitrogen cycle and so cause the extinction of life.

The nitrogen cycle is also very closely tied to the cyles of the elements carbon and oxygen. This subject is perhaps too technical to explore very far here, but the denitrifying bacteria do oxidize organic matter in the soil to get the energy for their activities. So there is a cycling of carbon that goes along with this nitrogen cycle, and there is also a cycle of oxygen involved.

The only reason we have oxygen in our atmosphere is that green plants keep putting it there. The plants take in carbon dioxide and give off oxygen. Animals and microorganisms take in oxygen and give off carbon dioxide; so do our factories, our furnaces, and our automobiles. Seventy percent of the free oxygen produced each year comes from planktonic diatoms in the oceans. But what thought does man give to the diatoms when he disposes of his waste? When he wants a new highway, factory, housing project, or strip mine, he is not even solicitous of the plants growing on land. The fate of Lake Erie and many lesser bodies of water has shown us that man is capable of blocking the oxygen cycle by sheer carelessness .

If this leaves you complacent, let me mention just a few other details. The deciduous forests of the eastern United States appear to produce about 1000 times as much oxygen per unit area as the average cover of the earth's surface. Yet, forests seem to be the first resource that modern man is willing to dispense with. Tropical rain forests, unlike our deciduous forests, carry on photosynthesis throughout the year and so are probably considerably more productive. But several times each year I read of schemes for industrializing or "developing" the tropical regions of Latin America, Africa, and Asia. Recently, a Brazilian official issued a statement that his country must develop the Amazon basin. Tropical soils are typically low in mineral nutrients, and such minerals as are present leach from the soil quickly if the vegetation is unable to trap them and recycle them. Once a tropical forest is destroyed, the change may be irreversible.

I do not think any educated and responsible person would advocate applying defoliants and herbicides to a tropical forest without first making a careful survey of the nutrient status of the soil and vegetation. But ecological understanding is not a prerequisite for policy making.

The U.S. Commerce Department has ordered the suppliers to turn over the entire production of the so-called weed killer 2,4,5-T to the military for use in Vietnam. The military is also taking about a third of our production of weed killer 2,4-D for this purpose. It is taking the entire output of a really horrid new weed killer known as picloram. This is a very persistent chemical. There is one case in Vermont where mules ate vegetation that had been sprayed with picloram. Later, when the manure from the mules was used for fertilizer, it killed the plants it was put on. When picloram has been experimentally sprayed on a forest, typically no woody vegetation has grown for two years. The military is also about to let or may already have let, a major contract for increasing the production of picloram. Presumably, it is going to ship the chemical to Vietnam in tankers. What happens if a few of these tankers sink in the Pacific Ocean? I have seen no experimental data on the effects of picloram on marine diatoms, but I know what it does to terrestrial plants, and I find this a very disturbing project.

Similarly, in the seas, estuaries tend to be much more productive than either the land adjacent to them or most of the open ocean. In Georgia, figures show that the salt marshes and estuaries are two to three times as productive of life as the best agricultural land in the state. These estuaries not only produce oxygen but also serve as nursery grounds for the immature stages of species we harvest for sea food.

Yet, estuaries are where coastal man is likely to dump his refuse. They are the place where commercial developers constantly seek land fill and conduct dredging operations. They are also among the places where it is proposed to locate huge electrical generating plants which would raise the temperature of the water and, in some cases, pollute it with radioisotopes. But who is thinking of the welfare of these green plants or the organisms involved in the nitrogen cycle or of still additional types of organisms which are essential for man's survival?

Perhaps I should mention one more type of organism. Photosynthesis varies tremendously in time and place; it stops at night and, on land areas in high latitudes, it practically stops during the winter, and it is slowed down in other areas by seasonal drought and other factors. Similarly, our oxidative processes vary extremely in time and space. How can these two rates be kept equal? There has to be a governor somewhere in the system, some feedback mechanism that will release more oxygen as oxygen content starts to fall and vice versa.

We wondered for a long time where this governor was. We suspect now that at least a very important part of it may be in the sulfate-reducing bacteria which occupy oxygen-free environments on the bottoms of lakes, oceans, swamps, and similar places. A number of types of organisms obtain the energy for their activities by oxidizing sulfur to sulfate. When this sulfate is carried down into anaerobic environments, these sulfate-reducing bacteria reduce it to sulfide and conserve oxygen in the process. This is the source of the hydrogen sulfide that comes bubbling off highly polluted bodies of water; it is the source of spherules of metallic pyrites, which are sulfides found by taking the sediment out of a swamp or a lake and examining it microscopically.

As a corollary of our rapid use of oxygen and our threats to the species that produce it, we are adding carbon dioxide to the atmosphere more rapidly than the oceans can assimilate it. This has serious implications for changing the climates of the earth, but the details of what may happen are still uncertain and controversial.

I would like to put one point in the form of a question: Would any rational creature go on changing his environment like this without understanding the possible effects, and at the same time argue that it is necessary to keep the destructive process expanding each year? What is now popularly known as progress begins to look very much like the path toward extinction.

I have attempted some quantitative calculations for the oxygen cycle in order to see where we stand. For the 48 conterminous United States I took the 1966 figures for production and import of fossil fuels. I corrected these for exports and for noncombustible residues and then calculated the amount of oxygen it would take to burn them. Then I made what I believe is the best possible estimate of the amount of oxygen that could be produced within the 48 conterminous states by photosynthesis in that same year. The figure for production of oxygen turned out to be not 60 percent of that for consumption.

The implication is absolutely clear. We are completely dependent on atmospheric circulation to bring to us oxygen produced outside of our borders. This oxygen is most probably produced in the Pacific Ocean. Think again about those tankers carrying picloram to the Far East. If we should seriously attempt to industrialize all of the nations of the earth after our own pattern, I think we would all perish for lack of oxygen long before the transition was near completion.

I've been discussing the atmosphere without unnatural contaminants. There is no secret about the true situation—that over 3000 foreign chemicals have been identified in our atmosphere; that in our cities, particulate matter (soot, fly ash, and, perhaps more importantly, particles of asbestos from brakes and of rubber from tires) pose a health problem; that carbon monoxide, sulfur dioxide, and various nitrogen oxides pose many problems.

Our intense agricultural efforts to produce more food for ourselves raise problems. A few years ago I had a son in college out in Iowa, and at the end of the school year when I went out to pick him up, there was an interesting controversy running in the papers: a lawsuit in which one contingent was arguing that 2,4-D should be considered a normal part of the Iowa atmosphere during summer.

In Florida, and more recently in Montana and some of the other western states, the factories that produce phosphate fertilizer have caused severe problems. Phosphorus is in such short supply that it is going to be the first chemical to run out for man, unless we can learn to mine it from the ocean bottoms. All living things are dependent on phosphorus for their survival. I have already mentioned the way we are throwing it away in detergents, and still it is so necessary to have phosphate fertilizers that we permit severe environmental damage around the industrial buildings that produce them.

In producing the super phosphate fertilizer, tremendous amounts of fluorine are given off into the atmosphere. Fluorine is very toxic to vegetation; it kills the plants growing around or downwind from the phosphate factories. There have been a number of lawsuits involving the death of livestock that have eaten plants polluted with fluorine. In one case in Florida, the plaintiffs were trying to force a manufacturer to put on higher stacks. Of course, this would not reduce the pollution; it would only spread it a little more widely. The company argued that fluorine is so corrosive that it was not practicable to put on higher stacks because the stacks would corrode too rapidly. The company won the suit. So now human lungs are being asked to assimilate something that brick and mortar cannot cope with.

There has been quite a bit published about new prospects for turning petroleum and coal directly into food for man through the activities of various bacteria, yeasts, and fungi. It is a sad fact that the metabolism of bacteria, yeasts, and fungi does not liberate oxygen.

It may be instructive to consider one pollutant in detail in order to appreciate the widespread nature of our problem. I think I could make just as good a story of arsenic, but I have chosen to discuss lead. I have already mentioned the ancient smelting operations in Britain in Roman times. When the lead had been transported to Rome, it went into paint, into water pipes, and to line the vessels used for storing wine. (Apparently, a lead taste is preferable to a bronze taste.) Recent studies of Roman bones have found concentrations of lead which indicate that many members of the upper classes must have suffered from lead poisoning. It has been suggested that this may have contributed to the decline of the empire.

Until recently in this country, lead was a constituent of indoor paint. Lead arsenate was a favorite insecticide, especially for use on tobacco. It got into the soil, and so now we inhale lead with our tobacco smoke. In our city slums, children suffer mental retardation and even die from lead in peeling paint they have eaten. New York City had 509 reported cases in 1964, and the number is steadily rising as more physicians become aware of the problem and capable of diagnosing lead poisoning.

The burning of ethyl gasoline in our cars is putting tremendous quantities of lead into the atmosphere. This is literally polluting much of the world. A recent study of old elm trees has shown rapidly rising concentrations of lead in the wood produced since 1937. A study of snow near the North Pole has shown a 300 percent increase in lead content since 1940. Antarctica is still relatively uncontaminated, but you can detect lead in the snow there. The air over the tropical Pacific contains less lead than that over rural America, although the lead is still present.

Let me seem to digress to consider a very different topic which will, however, bring us back to the problem of lead in the environment. We hear a great deal of talk today about increasing food production from the sea, but any substantial increase will have to come from subtropical and tropical waters. Indeed, many of the sea food populations in higher latitudes are suffering from overexploitation today. In tropical and subtropical waters, especially around islands, there occurs a mysterious type of sea food poisoning known as ciguatera. Fish that have been wholesome food may suddenly become poisonous to man. Or fish on one side of an island may be good to eat, while the same species on the other side of the island is deadly. Apparently, any kind of fish can be involved, including such food staples as anchovies, sardines, and herrings; such sportsmen's favorites as bonefish and sailfish; and such gourmets' delights as pompano and red snapper. Rarely, outbreaks have been attributed to shellfish such as crabs and lobsters. Sometimes, nearly all of the victims recover; in other outbreaks, nearly all die. Nobody knows what causes ciguatera, but I would like to suggest that pollution by man may be involved. It may at least trigger outbreaks.

On the day after Christmas in 1964, the British freighter *Southbank* was wrecked at Washington Island about 1000 miles south of Hawaii. Ciguatera had never been reported there. Salvage crews went to work, and they frequently caught and ate fish. Then, in August 1965, *Southbank* sank completely, for the first time flooding the main cargo hold. In that same month the fish became poisonous, and those who ate them were taken violently ill. Lead is known to have constituted part of the cargo.

I would not be so rash as to state categorically that lead is the cause of ciguatera. If this should happen to be the case, however, I think it would be ironic that growth of the automotive industry should decrease the potential for food production thousands of miles away. Meanwhile, the lead in exhaust gases is interfering with the attempts of chemists to devise ways of reducing concentrations of other pollutants. There is mounting evidence, which I cannot evaluate, that lead and other heavy metals may play a role in causing cancer.

Obviously, the problem at the base of all the other problems is excessive population growth. Man has been on earth for at least a million years. By the beginning of the Christian era, he numbered perhaps 5,000,000 persons. His population had been doubling about once every 50,000 years. In the summer of 1968 the human population of the world passed the 3.5 billion mark. If the present trend continues, it will continue to double about every 35 years. There is no possibility that the earth can continue to support such growth. In fact, it is very doubtful that the earth is capable of supporting on a sustained basis a population as large as the present one.

I can think of nothing more important for man to do than to bring the world's best minds to bear on these questions: How large a human population can the earth support indefinitely? How much industry of what kinds can be supported indefinitely? What kinds of contamination of the environment can be tolerated? How can waste be recycled? How can we conserve or reclaim our resources of minerals and energy sources?

We have the technology to regulate the population size. This could be done; but to solve our problems, we will have to call for cooperative efforts of biological scientists, physical scientists, sociologists, psychologists, economists, and political scientists. We must abandon our mania for continued expansion of everything. With so many groups necessarily involved, interaction of scientists with economists and political scientists, and so forth, I cannot feel very optimistic.

Make your own evaluation of our chances.

The Plight

Ian L. McHarg

Thirty years ago the wilderness of Scotland looked inviolate to me and I would have been content to give my life to the creation of oases of delight in the heart of Glasgow or dream of a marriage of man and nature in new cities and towns. My boyhood sense of the rest of the world suggested that it was even wilder than Scotland. There were still explorers in those days and missionaries enough to build a stamp collection from their solicitations. The plight that moved me then was little enough compared to today. Then there was no threat of an atomic holocaust and no fear of radiation hazard. The population problem was one of declining birthrates and Mussolini exhorted and coerced Italian mothers to greater efforts while Presidents of France deplored an effete generation. DDT and Dieldrin were not yet festering thoughts; penicillin and streptomycin were not yet hopes. Man's inhumanity to man was commonplace in distant lands but had not achieved the pinnacle of depravity which at Belsen and Dachau a civilized nation was to achieve. Poverty and oppression were real and pervasive, and war was imminent enough so that I could conclude at seventeen that I had better be ready as a trained soldier in 1939.

Yet while the city was grim indeed, the countryside could be reached by foot, by bicycle or even for the few pennies that led

Ian L. McHarg is professor and chairman of the Department of Landscape Architecture and Regional Planning which he founded at the University of Pennsylvania. As a landscape architect and regional planner, he and the firm Wallace, McHarg, Roberts and Todd have used ecological planning methods to make several celebrated studies, among them the Minneapolis-St. Paul Metropolitan Region, the I-95 and Richmond Parkway Studies, the Inner Harbor Plan for Baltimore, and the Lower Manhattan Plan. He is widely known as a TV personality and as a writer. This chapter was taken from his recent book, Design with Nature (New York, Doubleday, Natural History Press, 1969), since recording difficulties prevented reproduction of his lecture at the Yale School of Forestry.

to a tram terminus and the gateway to wild lands where no law of trespass constrained.

The country is not a remedy for the industrial city, but it does offer surcease and some balm to the spirit. Indeed, during the Depression there were many young men who would not submit to the indignity of the dole or its queues and who chose to live off the land, selling their strength where they could for food and poaching when they could not, sleeping in the bracken or a shepherd's bothy in good weather, living in hostels and public libraries in winter. They found independence, came to know the land and live from it, and sustained their spirit.

So, when first I encountered the problem of the place of nature in man's world it was not a beleaguered nature, but merely the local deprivation that was the industrial city. Scotland was wild enough, protected by those great conservators, poverty and inaccessibility. But this has changed dramatically in the intervening decades, so that today in Europe and the United States a great erosion has been accomplished which has diminished nature—not only in the countryside at large, but within the enlarging cities and, not least, in man as a natural being.

There are large numbers of urban poor for whom the countryside is known only as the backdrop to westerns or television advertisements. Paul Goodman speaks of poor children who would not eat carrots pulled from the ground because they were dirty, terror-stricken at the sight of a cow, who screamed in fear during a thunderstorm. The Army regularly absorbs young men who have not the faintest conception of living off the land, who know nothing of nature and its processes. In classical times the barbarians in fields and forest could only say "bar bar" like sheep; today their barbaric, sheepish descendants are asphalt men.

Clearly the problem of man and nature is not one of providing a decorative background for the human play, or even ameliorating the grim city: it is the necessity of sustaining nature as source of life, milieu, teacher, sanctum, challenge and, most of all, of rediscovering nature's corollary of the unknown in the self, the source of meaning.

There are still great realms of empty ocean, deserts reaching to the curvature of the earth, silent, ancient forests and rocky coasts, glaciers and volcanoes, but what will we do with them? There are rich contented farms, and idyllic villages, strong barns and white-steepled churches, tree-lined streets and covered bridges, but these are residues of another time. There are, too, the silhouettes of all the Manhattans, great and small, the gleaming golden windows of corporate images—expressionless prisms suddenly menaced by another of our creations, the supersonic transport whose sonic boom may reduce this image to a sea of shattered glass.

But what do we say now, with our acts in city and countryside? While I first addressed this question to Scotland in my youth, today the world directs the same question to the United States. What is our performance and example? What are the visible testaments to the American mercantile creed—the hamburger stand, gas station, diner, the ubiquitous billboards, sagging wires, the parking lot, car cemetery and that most complete conjunction of land rapacity and human disillusion, the subdivision. It is all but impossible to avoid the highway out of town, for here, arrayed in all its glory, is the quintessence of vulgarity, bedecked to give the maximum visibility to the least of our accomplishments.

And what of the cities? Think of the imprisoning gray areas that encircle the center. From here the sad suburb is an unrealizable dream. Call them no-place although they have many names. Race and hate, disease, poverty, rancor and despair, urine and spit live here in the shadows. United in poverty and ugliness, their symbol is the abandoned carcasses of automobiles, broken glass, alleys of rubbish and garbage. Crime consorts with disease, group fights group, the only emancipation is the parked car.

What of the heart of the city, where the gleaming towers rise from the dirty skirts of poverty? Is it like midtown Manhattan where twenty per cent of the population was found to be indistinguishable from the patients in mental hospitals? [1] Both stimulus and stress live here with the bitch goddess success. As you look at the faceless prisms do you recognize the home of *anomie.*

[1] Leo Srole, et al., *Mental Health in the Metropolis: The Midtown Manhattan Study* (New York, McGraw-Hill, 1962).

Can you find the river that first made the city? Look behind the unkempt industry, cross the grassy railroad tracks and you will find the rotting piers and there is the great river, scummy and brown, wastes and sewage bobbing easily up and down with the tide, endlessly renewed.

If you fly to the city by day you will see it first as a smudge of smoke on the horizon. As you approach, the outlines of its towers will be revealed as soft silhouettes in the hazardous haze. Nearer you will perceive conspicuous plumes which, you learn, belong to the proudest names in industry. Our products are household words but it is clear that our industries are not yet housebroken. Drive from the airport through the banks of gas storage tanks and the interminable refineries. Consider how dangerous they are, see their cynical spume, observe their ugliness. Refine they may, but refined they are not.

You will drive on an expressway, a clumsy concrete form, untouched by either humanity or art, testament to the sad illusion that there can be a solution for the unbridled automobile. It is ironic that this greatest public investment in cities has also financed their conquest. See the scars of the battle in the remorseless carving, the dismembered neighborhoods, the despoiled parks. Manufacturers are producing automobiles faster than babies are being born. Think of the depredations yet to be accomplished by myopic highway builders to accommodate these toxic vehicles. You have plenty of time to consider in the long peak hour pauses of spasmodic driving in the blue gas corridors.

You leave the city and turn towards the countryside. But can you find it? To do so you will follow the paths of those who tried before you. Many stayed to build. But those who did so first are now deeply embedded in the fabric of the city. So as you go you transect the rings of the thwarted and disillusioned who are encapsulated in the city as nature endlessly eludes pursuit.

You can tell when you have reached the edge of the countryside for there are many emblems—the cadavers of old trees piled in untidy heaps at the edge of the razed deserts, the magnificient machines for land despoliation, for felling forests, filling marshes, culverting streams, and sterilizing farmland, making thick brown sediments of the creeks.

Is this the countryside, the green belt—or rather the greed belt, where the farmer sells land rather than crops, where the developer takes the public resource of the city's hinterland and subdivides to create a private profit and a public cost? Certainly here is the area where public powers are weakest—either absent or elastic—where the future costs of streets, sidewalks and sewers, schools, police and fire protection are unspoken. Here are the meek mulcted, the refugees thwarted.

Rural land persists around the metropolis, not because we have managed the land more wisely but because it is larger, more resistant to man's smear, more resilient. Nature regenerates faster in the country than in the city where the marks of men are well-nigh irreversible. But it still wears the imprint of man's toil. DDT is in the arctic ice, in the ocean deeps, in the rivers and on the land, atomic wastes rest on the Continental Shelf, many creatures are forever extinguished, and the primeval forests have all but gone and only the uninitiated imagine that these third and fourth growth stands are more than shadows of their forebears. Although we can still see great fat farms, their once deep soils, a geological resource, are thinner now, and we might well know that farming is another kind of mining, dissipating the substance of aeons of summers and multitudes of life. The Mississippi is engorged with five cubic miles of soil each year, a mammoth prodigality in a starving world. Lake Erie is on the verge of becoming septic, New York City suffers from water shortages while the Hudson flows foully past, salt water encroaches in the Delaware, floods alternate with drought, the fruits of two centuries of land mismanagement. Forest fires, mudslides and smog become a way of life in Los Angeles, and the San Andreas Fault rises in temperature to menace San Franciscans.

The maps all show the continent to be green wild landscapes save for the sepia cities huddled on lakes and seaboards, but look from a plane as it crosses the continent and makes an idiocy of distance, see the wild green sectioned as rigorously as the city. In the great plains nature persists only in the meandering stream and the flood plain forest, a meaningful geometry in the Mondriaan patterns of unknowing men.

It matters not if you choose to proceed to the next city or return to the first. You can confirm an urban destination from the increased shrillness of the neon shills, the diminished horizon, the loss of nature's companions until you are alone, with men, in the heart of the city, God's Junkyard—or should it be called Bedlam, for cacophony lives here. It is the expression of the inalienable right to create ugliness and disorder for private greed, the maximum expression of man's inhumanity to man. And so our cities grow, coalescing into a continental necklace of megalopoles, dead gray tissue encircling the nation.

Surely the indictment is too severe—there must be redeeming buildings, spaces, places, landscapes. Of course there are—random chance alone would have ensured some successful accidents. But there are also positive affirmations, yet it is important to recognize that many of these are bequests from earlier times. Independence, Carpenter and Faneuil Hall symbolize the small but precious heritage of the 18th century: the great State Houses, city halls, museums, concert halls, city universities and churches, the great urban park systems, were products of the last century. Here in these older areas you will find humane, generous suburbs where spacious men built their concern into houses and spaces so that dignity and peace, safety and quiet live there, shaded by old trees, warmed by neighborliness.

You may also see hints of a new vitality and new forms in the cities, promising resurgence. You may even have found, although I have not, an expressway that gives structure to a city, or, as I have, a parkway that both reveals and enhances the landscape. There are farmlands in good heart; there are landowners—few it is true—who have decided that growth is inevitable, but that it need not lead to despoliation but to enlargement. New towns are being constructed and concepts of regional planning are beginning to emerge. There is an increased awareness for the need to manage resources and even a title for this concern—The New Conservation. There is a widening certainty that the Gross National Product does not measure health or happiness, dignity, compassion, beauty or delight, and that these are, if not all inalienable rights, at least most worthy aspirations.

But these are rare among the countless city slums and scabrous towns, pathetic subdivisions, derelect industries, raped land, befouled rivers and filthy air.

At the time of the founding of the republic—and for millennia before—the city had been considered the inevitable residence for the urbane, civilized and polite. Indeed all of these names *say* city. It was as widely believed that rich countries and empires were inevitably built upon the wealth of the land. The original cities and towns of the American 18th century were admirable— Charleston and Savannah, Williamsburg, Boston, Philadelphia, New Orleans. The land was rich and beautiful, canons of taste espoused the 18th-century forms of architecture and town building, a wonder of humanity and elegance.

How then did our plight come to be and what can be done about it? It is a long story which must be told briefly and, for that reason, it is necessary to use a broad brush and paint with coarse strokes. This method inevitably offends for it omits qualifying statements, employs broad generalities and often extrapolates from too slender evidence. Yet the basic question is so broad that one need not be concerned with niceties. The United States is the stage on which great populations have achieved emancipation from oppression, slavery, peonage and serfdom, where a heterogeneity of peoples has become one and where an unparalleled wealth has been widely distributed. These are the jewels of the American diadem. But the setting, the environment of this most successful social revolution, is a major indictment against the United States and a threat to her success and continued evolution.

Our failure is that of the Western World and lies in prevailing values. Show me a man-oriented society in which it is believed that reality exists only because man can perceive it, that the cosmos is a structure erected to support man on its pinnacle, that man exclusively is divine and given dominion over all things, indeed that God is made in the image of man, and I will predict the nature of its cities and their landscapes. I need not look far for we have seen them—the hot-dog stands, the neon shill, the ticky-tacky houses, dysgenic city and mined landscapes. This is the image of the anthropomorphic, anthropocentric man; he seeks not unity with nature but conquest. Yet unity he finally finds, but only when his arrogance and ignorance are stilled and he lies dead under the greensward. We need this unity to survive.

Among us it is widely believed that the world consists solely of a dialogue between men, or men and God, while nature is a faintly decorative backdrop to the human play. If nature receives attention, then it is only for the purpose of conquest, or even better, exploitation—for the latter not only accomplishes the first objective, but provides a financial reward for the conqueror.

We have but one explicit model of the world and that is built upon economics. The present face of the land of the free is its clearest testimony, even as the Gross National Product is the proof of its success. Money is our measure, convenience is its cohort, the short term is its span, and the devil may take the hindmost is the morality.

Perhaps there is a time and place for everything; and, with wars and revolutions, with the opening and development of continents, the major purposes of exploration and settlement override all lesser concerns and one concludes in favor of the enterprises while regretting the wastages and losses which are incurred in these extreme events. But if this was once acceptable as the inevitable way, that time has passed.

The pioneers, the builders of railroads and canals, the great industrialists who built the foundations for future growth were hard-driven, single-minded men. Like soldiers and revolutionaries, they destroyed much in disdain and in ignorance, but there are fruits from their energies and we share them today. Their successors, the merchants, are a different breed, more obsequious and insidious. The shock of the assassination of a President stilled for only one day their wheedling and coercive blandishments for our money. It is their ethos, with our consent, that sustains the slum-lord and the land rapist, the polluters of rivers and atmosphere. In the name of profit they preempt the seashore and sterilize the landscape, fell the great forests, fill the protective marshes, build cynically in the flood plain. It is the claim of convenience for commerce—or its illusion—that drives the expressway through neighborhoods, homes and priceless parks, a taximeter of indifferent greed. Only the merchant's creed can justify the slum as a sound investment or offer tomato stakes as the highest utility for the priceless and irreplaceable redwoods.

The economists, with a few exceptions, are the merchants' minions and together they ask with the most barefaced effrontery that we accommodate our value system to theirs. Neither love nor compassion, health nor beauty, dignity nor freedom, grace nor delight are important unless they can be priced. If they are non-price benefits or costs they are relegated to inconsequence. The economic model proceeds inexorably towards its self-fulfillment of more and more despoliation, uglification and inhibition to life, all in the name of progress—yet, paradoxically, the components which the model excludes are the most important human ambitions and accomplishments and the requirements for survival.

The origins of societies and of exchange go back to an early world when man was a minor inconsequence in the face of an overwhelming nature. He bartered his surpluses of food and hides, cattle, sheep and goats and valued scarcities, gold and silver, myrrh and frankincense. But the indispensable elements of life and survival were beyond his ken and control: they could not and did not enter his value system save imperfectly, through religious views. Nor have they yet. But in the intervening millennia the valuations attributed to commodities have increased in range and precision and the understanding of the operation of the limited sphere of economics has increased dramatically. This imperfect view of the world as commodity fails to evaluate and incorporate physical and biological processes: we have lost the empirical knowledge of our ancestors. We are now unable to attribute value to indispensable natural processes, but we have developed an astonishing precision for ephemera.

It is obvious that such an institutionalized myopic prejudice will exclude the realities of the biophysical world. Its very man-centeredness ensures that those processes, essential to man's evolution and survival, will be excluded from consideration and from evaluation. We have no thought in the interminable dialogues among men for the sustaining sun, the moon and tides, the oceans and hydrologic cyle, the inclined axis of the earth and the seasons. As a society we neither know nor value the chemical elements and compounds that constitute life, and their cycles, the importance of the photosynthetic plant, the essential decomposers, the ecosystems, their constituent organisms, their roles and cooperative mechanisms, the prodigality of life forms, or even that greatest of values, the genetic pool with which we confront the future.

Yet we may soon learn. Consider the moon. It apparently lacks an atmosphere and oceans and the great inheritance of life forms which we enjoy. The costs of "terra-farming" this naked, hostile planet to that benign condition which can support life as abundantly as does the earth are considered of such a magnitude as to be inconceivable. Colonies on the moon will thus have to be small envelopes enclosing some of the essential commonplaces of earth transported as priceless and indispensable commodities. The man on the moon will know the value of these things.

But surely we need not await the confrontation with the inhospitable moon to learn a lesson so rudimentary, so well known to our ancient ancestors and as familiar to the simple societies of the world today.

Economic determinism as an imperfect evaluation of the biophysical world is only one of the consequences of our inheritance. An even more serious deficiency is the attitude towards nature and man which developed from the same source and of which our economic model is only one manifestation. The early men who were our ancestors wielded much the same scale of power over nature which Australian aboriginals do today. They were generally pantheists, animatists or animists. They tried to understand the phenomenal world and through behavior, placation and sacrifice, diminish adversity and increase beneficence. This early empiricism remains a *modus vivendi* for many tribal peoples, notably the American Indian—and conspicuously the Pueblo—today.

Whatever the earliest roots of the western attitude to nature it is clear that they were confirmed in Judaism. The emergence of monotheism had as its corollary the rejection of nature; the af-firmation of Jehovah, the God in whose image man was made, was also a declaration of war on nature.

The great western religions born of monotheism have been the major source of our moral attitudes. It is from them that we have developed the preoccupation with the uniqueness of man, with justice and compassion. On the subject of man-nature, however, the Biblical creation story of the first chapter of Genesis, the source of the most generally accepted description of man's role and powers, not only fails to correspond to reality as we observe it, but in its insistence upon dominion and subjugation of nature, encourages the most exploitative and destructive instincts in man rather than those that are deferential and creative. Indeed, if one seeks license for those who would increase radioactivity, create canals and harbors with atomic bombs, employ poisons without constraint, or give consent to the bulldozer mentality, there could be no better injunction than this text. Here can be found the sanction and injunction to conquer nature—the enemy, the threat to Jehovah.

The creation story in Judaism was absorbed unchanged into Christianity. It emphasized the exclusive divinity of man, his God-given dominion over all things and licensed him to subdue the earth. While Abraham Heschel, Gustave Weigel, and Paul Til-lich, speaking for Judaism and Christianity, reject the literality of this view and insist that it is an allegory, it is abundantly clear that it is the literal belief that had and does permeate the western view of nature and man. When this is understood, the conquest, the depredations and the despoliation are comprehensible, as is the imperfect value system.

From early, faintly ridiculous beginnings when a few inconse-quential men proclaimed their absolute supremacy to an unhear-ing and uncaring world, this theme has grown. It had only a modest place in classical Greece, where it was tempered by a parallel pantheism. It enlarged during the Roman tenure but was also subject to the same constraints. When the Millennium passed without punishment it grew more confident. In the Humanism of the Renaissance it made a gigantic leap and it is somewhat poignant that the poverty of the Mediterranean today is a product of the land mismanagement that occurred during this great inflation of the human ego and the increase of man's powers over nature. The 18th century was a period of pause—the Naturalist view emerged—but it barely arrested the anthropomorphic, anthropocentric surge that swelled in the 19th century and is our fullblown inheritance today.

The Inquisition was so outraged by doubt cast upon the primacy of man and his planet that Galileo was required to rescind his certainty that the earth revolved around the sun. This same insistence upon human divinity takes hard the evidence of man's animal ancestry or indeed the history of evolution. It looks as if it will resist the evidence that man's pre-hominid ancestors might well have been feral killers whose evolutionary success can be attributed to this capacity.

If the highest values in a culture insist that man must subdue the earth and that this is his moral duty, it is certain that he will in time acquire the powers to accomplish that injunction. It is not that man has produced evidence for his exclusive divinity, but only that he has developed those powers that permit the fulfillment of his aggressive destructive dreams. He now can extirpate great realms of life: he is the single agent of evolutionary regression.

In times long past, when man represented no significant power to change nature, it mattered little to the world what views he held. Today, when he has emerged as potentially the most destructive force in nature and its greatest exploiter, it matters very much indeed. One looks to see whether with the acquisition of knowledge and powers the western attitudes to nature and to man in nature have changed. But for all of modern science it is still pre-Copernican man whom we confront. He retains the same implicit view of exclusive divinity, man apart from nature, dominant, exhorted to subdue the earth—be he Jew, Christian or agnostic.

Yet surely this is an ancient deformity, an old bile of vengeance that we can no longer tolerate. This view neither approximates reality nor does it help us towards our objectives of survival and evolution. One longs for a world psychiatrist who could assure the patient that expressions of his cultural inferiority are no longer necessary or appropriate. Man is now emancipated, he can stand erect among the creatures. His ancient vengeance, a product of his resentment at an earlier insignificance, is obsolete. He exercises great destructive powers, less worthy of adulation than creative skills but enough for the moment to assuage the yearnings for primacy so long denied. From his position of destructive eminence he can now look to his mute partners and determine who they are, what they are, what they do, and realistically appraise the system within which he lives—his role, his dependencies—and reconstitute a cosmography that better accords with the world he experiences and which sustains him.

For me the indictment of city, suburb, and countryside becomes comprehensible in terms of the attitudes to nature that society has and does espouse. These environmental degradations are the inevitable consequence of such views. It is not incongruous but inevitable that the most beautiful landscapes and the richest farmlands should be less highly valued than the most scabrous slum and loathsome roadside stand. Inevitably an anthropocentric society will choose tomato stakes as a higher utility than the priceless and irreplaceable redwoods they have supplanted.

Where you find a people who believe that man and nature are indivisible, and that survival and health are contingent upon an understanding of nature and her processes, these societies will be very different from ours, as will be their towns, cities and landscapes. The hydraulic civilizations, the good farmer through time, the vernacular city builders have all displayed this acuity. But it is in the traditional society of Japan that the full integration of this view is revealed. That people, as we know, has absorbed a little of the best of the West and much of the worst while relinquishing accomplishments that we have not yet attained and can only envy.

In that culture there was sustained an agriculture at once incredibly productive and beautiful, testimony to an astonishing acuity to nature. This perception is reflected in a language rich in descriptive power in which the nuances of natural processes, the tilth of the soil, the dryness of wind, the burgeoning seed, are all precisely describable. The poetry of this culture is rich and succinct, the graphic arts reveal the landscape as the icon. Architecture, village and town building use natural materials directly with stirring power, but it is garden making that is the unequaled art form of this society. The garden is the metaphysical symbol of society in Tao, Shinto and Zen—man in nature.

Yet this view is not enough: man has fared less well than nature here. The jewel of the western tradition is the insistence upon the uniqueness of the individual and the preoccupation with justice and compassion. The Japanese medieval feudal view has been casual to the individual human life and rights. The western assumption of superiority has been achieved at the expense of nature. The oriental harmony of man-nature has been achieved at the expense of the individuality of man. Surely a united duality can be achieved by accounting for man as a unique individual rather than as a species, man in nature.

Let us by all means honor the attribution of dignity, even divinity, to man. But do we need to destroy nature to justify man—or even to obtain God's undivided attention? We can only be enlarged by accepting the reality of history and seeing ourselves in a non-human past, our survival contingent upon non-human processes. The acceptance of this view is not only necessary for the emancipation of western man, it is essential for the survival of all men.

If the Orient is the storehouse of the art of naturalism, it is the West that is the repository of anthropocentric art. It is a great if narrow inheritance, a glorious wealth of music and painting, sculpture and architecture. The Acropolis and Saint Peter, Autun and Beauvais, Chartres and Chambord, Ely and Peterborough—all speak of the divinity of man. But when the same views are extended and used as the structure for urban form, their illusory basis is revealed. The cathedral as the stage for a dialogue between man and God is admirable as a metaphysical symbol. When the supremacy of man is expressed in the form of the city, one seeks the evidence to support this superiority and finds only an assertion. Moreover, the insistence upon the divinity of man over

nature has as its companion the insistence in the divine supremacy of some man over all men. It requires a special innocence to
delight in the monumental accomplishments of the Renaissance
cities, notably Rome and Paris, without appreciating that the
generating impulses were more authoritarian than humanitarian—
authoritarian towards nature and man.

If we lower the eyes from the wonderful, strident but innocent
assertions of man's supremacy, we can find another tradition,
more pervasive than the island monuments, little responsive to
the grand procession of architectural styles. This is the vernacular
tradition. The empiricist may not know first principles, but he
has observed relations between events—he is not a victim of
dogma. The farmer is the prototype. He prospers only insofar as
he understands the land and by his management maintains its
bounty. So too with the man who builds. If he is perceptive to
the processes of nature, to materials and to forms, his creations
will be appropriate to the place; they will satisfy the needs of
social process and shelter, be expressive and endure. As indeed
they have, in the hill towns of Italy, the island architecture of
Greece, the medieval communities of France and the Low Countries and, not least, the villages of England and New England.

Two widely divergent views have been discussed, the raucous
anthropocentrism which insists upon the exclusive divinity of
man, his role of dominion and subjugation on one hand, and the
oriental view of man submerged in nature on the other. Each view
has distinct advantages, both have adaptive value. Are the benefits
of each mutually exclusive? I think not? but in order to achieve
the best of both worlds it is necessary to retreat from polar
extremes. There is indisputable evidence that man exists in nature; but it is important to recognize the uniqueness of the individual and thus his especial opportunities and responsibilities.

If the adaptation of the western view towards this more en-
compassing attitude required the West to accept Tao, Shinto or
Zen, there would be little hope for any transformation. However,
we have seen that the vernacular of the West has many similarities
to the products of oriental pantheism. There is another great
bridge, the 18th-century English landscape tradition. This move-

ment originated in the poets and writers of the period, from whom developed the conception of a harmony of man and nature. The landscape image was derived from the painters of the Campagna—Claude Lorraine, Salvator Rosa and Poussin. It was confirmed in a new aesthetic by the discovery of the Orient and on these premises transformed England from a poverty-stricken and raddled land to that beautiful landscape that still is visible today. This is a valid western tradition, it presumes a unity of man and nature, it was developed empirically by a few landscape architects, it accomplished a most dramatic transformation, it has endured. Yet the precursory understanding of natural processes that underlay it was limited. A better source is that uniquely western preoccupation, science.

Surely the minimum requirement today for any attitude to man-nature is that it approximate reality. One could reasonably expect that if such a view prevailed, not only would it affect the value system, but also the expressions accomplished by society.

Where else can we turn for an accurate model of the world and ourselves but to science? We can accept that scientific knowledge is incomplete and will forever be so, but it is the best we have and it has that great merit, which religions lack, of being self-correcting. Moreover, if we wish to understand the phenomenal world, then we will reasonably direct our questions to those scientists who are concerned with this realm—the natural scientists More precisely, when our preoccupation is with the interaction of organisms and environment—and I can think of no better description for our concern—then we must turn to ecologists, for that is their competence.

We will agree that science is not the only mode of perception—that the poet, painter, playwright and author can often reveal in metaphor that which science is unable to demonstrate. But, if we seek a workman's creed which approximates reality and can be used as a model of the world and ourselves, then science does provide the best evidence.

From the ecological view one can see that, since life is only transmitted by life, then, by living, each one of us is physically linked to the origins of life and thus—literally, not metaphorically—to all life. Moreover, since life originated from matter then, by living, man is physically united back through the evolution of matter to the primeval hydrogen. The planet Earth has been the one home for all of its processes and all of its myriad inhabitants since the beginning of time, from hydrogen to men. Only the bathing sunlight changes. Our phenomenal world contains our origins, our history, our milieu; it is our home. It is in this sense that ecology (derived from *oikos*) is the science of the home.

George Wald once wrote facetiously that "it would be a poor thing to be an atom in a Universe without physicists. And physicists are made of atoms. A physicist is the atom's way of knowing about atoms." [2] Who knows what atoms yearn to be, but we are their progeny. It would be just as sad to be an organism in a universe without ecologists, who are themselves organisms. May not the ecologist be the atom's way of learning about organisms—and ours?

The ecological view requires that we look upon the world, listen and learn. The place, creatures and men were, have been, are now and are in the process of becoming. We and they are here now, co-tenants of the phenomenal world, united in its origins and destiny.

As we contemplate the squalid city and the pathetic subdivision, suitcase agriculture and the cynical industrialist, the insidious merchant, and the product of all these in the necklace of megalopoles around the continent, their entrails coalescing, we fervently hope that there is another way. There is. The ecological view is the essential component in the search for the face of the land of the free and the home of the brave. This work seeks to persuade to that effect. It consists of borrowings from the thoughts and dreams of other men, forged into a workman's code—an ecological manual for the good steward who aspires to art.

[2] George Wald in *The Fitness of the Environment,* by Lawrence J. Henderson (Boston, Beacon Press, 1958), p. xxiv.

Weather Modification in the Service of Mankind: Promise or Peril?

David Gates

The planet earth is a finite and unique ecosystem, immersed in the solar wind, bombarded by particles from space, and irradiated by sunlight. It is at the most advantageous distance from the sun for the support of life. If it were farther from the sun it would have a lower mean planetary temperature; closer in, it would be warmer. Its magnetic field shields organisms on the earth and deflects high-speed ionizing particles from the sun and from the cosmos. It is important to note that not all planets have magnetic fields such as our own. When there is no magnetic field, many of the energetic particles from the sun can bombard the atmosphere, causing showers of other atomic fragments and greatly increasing the intensity of ionizing particles at the surface.

What I am trying to say is that this business of life, evolution, and man is the consequence of a large number of converging factors, many things happening uniquely. I happen to believe that life does exist on other planets in the universe; it would be remarkable if it did not. Nevertheless, this convergence of all the right factors and the incredible symbiosis between life on earth and the character of the atmosphere, which went hand in hand in allowing higher organisms to evolve, is unusual.

We depend upon plants for oxygen, but there was a day far back in geologic times when the earth's atmosphere was much

David M. Gates is director of the Missouri Botanical Garden and professor of botany at Washington University in St. Louis, Missouri. After gaining fame as a physicist and authority on solar radiation and the optical properties of earth's atmosphere, he turned his interest to botany and biophysical ecology. He has served in many public agencies, among them the U.S. Public Health Service Advisory Committee for Clean Air Standards and the Public Health Affairs Committee of the Ecological Society of America, and has been an adviser to the U.S. Air Force Air Defense Command and the Air Pollution Foundation of Los Angeles.

more transparent to ultraviolet radiation. It did not have ozone in the stratosphere; it did not have oxygen in the atmosphere; it did not have plants on the surface to produce the oxygen. When plants first came out of the ocean where they were to some degree protected and screened from ultraviolet radiation, they began to release oxygen through photosynthesis. That oxygen set up a screen which began to encourage further plant growth. Evolution went on its course. An understanding of these relationships of the earth's ecosystem is essential to a discussion of weather modification.

The earth's ecosystem is a giant thermodynamic machine which—driven by sunlight—slowly evolved over a billion years or so. Primitive man caused slight changes in the cycle of life and the stability of ecosystems; modern man now is capable of creating changes with worldwide implications. Man, the rational animal, has often behaved impulsively and irrationally. With a growing population and a crowded planet, he now faces the consequences of his irresponsibility.

Man must exploit, but he can manage his environment in a highly intelligent manner. The real question is: Will he?

Anyone who suggests that man should not exploit is unrealistic. This is the way we live. This is the way we are, the way we have accomplished our technological status, the way we have developed our type of civilization and released ourselves from the drudgery of a bare existence, the way we have broken free to reach out for creative and cultural things. But we must exploit conservatively; we must exploit with rationale. We must understand what we are doing.

Inadvertent climate change—how much of this has been going on? To tamper with something unfamiliar and not know what you are doing is extreme folly. To tamper with the balance of the earth's ecosystem and not understand the causes and consequences is sheer suicide. Yet, this is precisely what mankind persists in doing.

Could man have done otherwise? Probably not. Man's capacity to change systems is so enormous that the inevitability of inadvertent change is a positive consequence. Nevertheless, the better we recognize what we are doing to the ecosystem, the better our chances become for intelligent management of the world and for a sustained quality of living.

For a number of years we have been told of a warming trend to the mean temperature of the earth between 1885 and 1940, an increase of about $.5°C$ or $.9°F$. The globe's mean winter temperature climbed $.9°C$ during that period. The mean annual temperature for the latitude belt from $40°$ to $70°$ North rose by $.9°C$. This means half a degree for the whole earth. Shortly after 1940, a very steep cooling trend set in.

The usual explanation for the warming trend was the effect exerted on the heat balance by the release of carbon dioxide (CO_2) through the burning of fossil fuels. A carbon dioxide increase *did* occur; there is ample evidence of it. Very good measurements were made during the International Geophysical Year (a five-year period) substantiating these increases. Some measurements were made on Hawaii's steep volcanic mountain, Mauna Loa, above the forest level and above the level of the trade-wind inversion, presumably where the air is pretty well mixed. Others were made in Antarctica, far from industrial sources, and in the Indian Ocean. The figures all agree and show a definite annual increase of carbon dioxide.

It takes about 1000 years for the vapor pressure of carbon dioxide in the atmosphere to come into equilibrium with the vapor pressure of CO_2 in the oceans. This is an important figure, because our lifetimes are comparatively short and our actions are impulsive by comparison. The things that we and our children and their children do are still of the order of 100 years. We are talking about changes of the earth's ecosystem due to *our* impact; they are small in time compared to the 1000 years that it takes for the carbon dioxide levels of the atmosphere to adjust to a change. During the single century from 1850 to 1950, the carbon dioxide content of the atmosphere increased yearly by 3.2 percent. When expressed as a percentage of the CO_2 concentration in 1950, the amount of carbon dioxide produced in 1962 was about 25 times the annual production back in 1850.

The rate of increase of atmospheric carbon dioxide due to the burning of fossil fuels is clearly speeding up. If that rate continues, by the year 2000 an additional 60 percent of carbon dioxide will have been injected into the earth's atmosphere. The amount in 1950 was roughly 300 parts per million by volume.

This may have a notable effect on surface temperature: an increase of several degrees in mean temperature and a decrease of several degrees in stratospheric temperatures. In reference to increased carbon dioxide, the term "greenhouse effect" is often used. That is basically an invalid description, because a greenhouse does a completely different thing; it shields plants from the wind.

Actually, the carbon dioxide of the atmosphere lets sunlight through because it does not have absorption bands in that part of the spectrum. But it does screen thermal radiation from the earth. Because it is black in certain bands, it is strongly absorbing at the wave lengths where the earth's surface radiates. So it absorbs; then it re-radiates, but in both directions from a mean temperature of the atmosphere which was colder than the ground surface temperature. If you could throw a blanket over the surface which is sending a lot of radiation back to space, the blanket would absorb some of that radiation and then re-radiate it in both directions at a lower temperature. You get some back, and you lose a smaller fraction to space. This is the reason for a warming caused by increased carbon dioxide.

Man is throwing other compounds into the air. He is putting great masses of dust into the atmosphere from the cities. The urban masses of concrete and asphalt are warmer, drier, and dustier than the country. The city may be ten to 20 times dustier than the countryside. The dust reflects sunlight to space and reduces the radiant energy absorbed by the ground, energy which would otherwise warm the surface.

Jet aircraft thread the skies and converge on airports located in or near the large cities. Through combustion they spew out great masses of water vapor and seed the sky with jet contrails which spread into broad bands of cirrus clouds, again adding to the reflection of sunlight into space. (On takeoff one kind of jet engine spews out 88 pounds of pollutants.) These cirrus clouds, these thin veils, these wisps of clouds formed by jet contrails, often spread out and persist. On cloudy days they do not make much difference; but on pleasant days when the atmosphere would naturally remain clear, this seeding of the skies adds to the cloud cover and to the reflection of light back into space.

Looking at all of these activities by men, we might blame ourselves for the cooling trend of the last two or three decades. But is it possible that the trend is unrelated to the dust and the contrails in the sky? Hurd C. Willett of the Massachusetts Institute of Technology has a theory of cyclical climate change which relates to sunspots with a 40-year period of warm and dry weather during high sunspot activity, followed by 40 years of relatively cold and rainy weather during periods of less sunspot activity. Dr. Willett says that we are in a cool period now with the coldest part to last from 1975 to 1995.

Is the cyclic climatic change linked to sunspots the only transition we have witnessed during the last century? Is this what we are saying? Can we conclude that the man-made pollution gathering in the skies has little to do with it? I doubt it, and many other scientists doubt it. Nevertheless, it is extremely difficult to prove cause and effect with a giant hydrodynamic, thermodynamic machine as complex as the earth's ecosystem of ground and atmosphere.

What about the great cities where so many of us live? It is self-evident that the climate of a city is very different from the climate of the country. The city has up to 30 percent less sunlight and 90 percent less ultraviolet radiation. The city has much more fog than the surrounding countryside. Saarbrucken, Germany, and Paris, France, are nearly five times foggier than the country nearby. It rains more in the city than in the country and, in fact, more in the city on weekdays than on Sundays.

This brings to mind the famous La Porte, Indiana, case history. The Gary steel mills seed the skies with fine particulates, and 50 miles downwind at La Porte their effect is felt in cloudy and wet days. There is an increase over the average of something like 230 percent in hailstorms, 31 percent in rainfall, and a comparable frequency in cloudy weather. It is a well-documented situation and a dramatic demonstration that inadvertent seeding of the skies with particulate matter can affect the climate.

High-compression automobile engines require the use of tetra-ethyl lead in gasoline to prevent knocking. After burning, fine particles of lead oxide are released into the atmosphere from automobile exhausts. If small amounts of iodine are in the atmosphere at the same time, they coat the fine lead oxide particles with less than a monolayer of iodine, and produce superb nuclei for ice crystal formation. A snowstorm may result. Where does the iodine come from? Some comes from the burning of fossil fuels; some is released by plants. Some is a residue of soil particles from burning seaweed, from processing natural nitrates; it is an effluent of some nuclear reactors; and, of course, it comes from the operation of silver iodide generators.

The practice of slash-and-burn agriculture adds enormous amounts of carbon dioxide and dust to the atmosphere. Large sections of Africa are obscured by smoke from fires intended to clear the land for agriculture. In fact, some travelers say that if you fly over Africa and expect to see the countryside, forget it; it is all haze. This practice, along with decaying vegetable matter in the humus zones of the world, is thought to produce much more CO_2 in the atmosphere than the burning of fossil fuels.

We must be very careful in our thinking on one point. It is true that the decay of vegetable matter can throw into the air much carbon dioxide and that vegetation may be releasing turpines and other volatiles into the atmosphere. We should not use that to claim that our own pollution of the atmosphere is any less significant, because the products of our impulsiveness are added to a biological system that has gone on slowly for millions of years.

If the earth's atmosphere were to warm for any reason, the release of carbon dioxide from plant respiration would increase, and the CO_2 concentration would increase; again, the implications of a warmer climate would be there. The change in the atmosphere's dust content can cause some effect on the climate; more sunlight is reflected back to space and more long-wave radiation retained on earth.

How much has the dust content of the earth changed over the

last few decades? Robert McCormick and John Ludwig of the Environmental Science Services Administration (ESSA) in Cincinnati have shown that the turbidity of the air—dustiness—increased 57 percent over Washington, D.C., in about 60 years and 88 percent over Davos, Switzerland, over 30 years. If you have been in Davos, it is sickening to think of that clean alpine air becoming 88 percent dustier. Reid Bryson of the Meteorology Department of the University of Wisconsin estimates that in ten years the dustiness over Hawaii's Mauna Loa Observatory, which is far from pollution sources, has increased 30 percent.

The earth's dustiness appears to have increased substantially during the last few decades. A turbidity, or dustiness, change of 3 to 4 percent, averaged over the whole planet, would change the earth's mean temperature by .4°C. The changes in turbidity will do something to worldwide climate, but the big question is what. Reid Bryson believes that the increased turbidity in the atmosphere from volcanic activity, dust storms, and man's pollution has overshadowed the carbon dioxide increase and is producing a cooling trend in the global climate. On the other hand, it could produce a warming trend. The dangerous thing is that we do not really know.

I have often wondered about a region in which I spent many summers—northern Michigan, where pioneers settled more than 100 years ago. Those early settlers began to slash and burn and wipe out the great deciduous and coniferous forests of that area, the contact zone between the woodland of the north and the timberland of the south. They did a thorough job, totally destroying the forests there. Because of the slash on the ground and the scrub that grew in place of the trees, fires swept over the territory.

That was before the public developed a conscience about fire regulation. My father and a friend reported (about 1919) seeing nine fires in seven miles. During my boyhood, when I played in the sand of northern Michigan in the summer, I got dirty because the sand was full of charcoal. It is still true today; those sands are suffused with the charcoal of utter devastation by our forefathers. I have often wondered: When settlers came into such a region and removed the great, green cathedral-like forests, putting in their place scrub and charcoal and exposing soil and sand, did they change the climate? Did their handiwork have any impact on the global climate?

Of course, they changed the microclimate dramatically. The climate of that exposed surface was totally different from the previous climate. It became hotter, drier, windier. But was this effect noticed any place else? Did it reflect on the climate to the east of that despoiled area? Those great fires of the upper peninsula cast dust all over the eastern United States; that must have attenuated the sunlight and affected the radiation.

When man plowed the prairies, replacing the grasslands with agriculture, did he affect the climate beyond the scene of his activities? The crops are not green and growing all year. When man plows, and exposes dark soil, and imposes on the soil the annual cycle of greening, harvesting, and plowing, does that affect the climate? Surely this has a large-scale effect over a vast region, compared with the normal ecosystem—even with fires in that normal ecosystem.

Do the highways that lace America affect the global climate? What are the consequences of paving vast areas of the North American continent with cement and asphalt? This substantially changes the albedo (the reflectants of sunlight). One meteorologist has suggested paving large surfaces in some parts of the earth with asphalt to create massive thermal updrafts of hot air which would produce artificial clouds and, thus, increase rainfall.

Man has intentionally modified the microclimate since he first put a house over his head or a barn over his cattle. He consciously modifies the climate when he mulches his crops or when he plants a shelter belt row of trees. In the early 1940s, Vincent Schaefer discovered that clouds could be seeded by sprinkling dry ice into supersaturated air. A short while later, Bernard Vonnegut found that silver iodide could also be used in cloud seeding. Many claims have been made for and against the effectiveness of these techniques. Today, dry ice is being tried experimentally to dissipate supercool clouds over airfields. It has been used successfully at a number of air bases, including the airport at Salt Lake City. However, it is not yet a generally adopted practice. Fogs over non-freezing basins of water are being averted by the spreading of fatty alcohol compounds on the surface of the water to retard evaporation, thus preventing the fog from forming. This is definite weather modification.

For about ten years, very careful studies have been made of the effectiveness of cloud seeding. According to a report by the National Academy of Sciences, seeding orographic storms (storms that rise because of the topography, normally a mountain range) with ground-base silver iodide has increased precipitation some 10 percent. Silver-iodide seeding of cumulus and other cloud types in the eastern United States has also produced about a 10 to 20 percent increase in precipitation.

In any event, cloud seeding neither terminates nor produces droughts. There is a great deal of legal protest over cloud seeding, much of it based on hearsay and emotion, but it has been exceedingly difficult to prove or to demonstrate its effects. Yet, some effects are noticeable; it is a useful technique, and it will improve. A modification of hurricanes by cloud seeding may be possible, but that is still in a strictly experimental stage. In the USSR rockets were used to introduce crystallizing agents into hailstorms from 1964 to 1967, thus reducing hail damage by 75 percent or more; both silver iodide and lead iodide were used in a total of 120 experiments. In Kenya, seeding agents in explosive rockets reduced hail damage by more than 50 percent.

Ten years ago Harry Wexler of the United States Weather Bureau suggested some ways of modifying weather on a large scale. His schemes were based on changing the radiation balance of the earth's surface. Two streams of radiant energy, one downward and the other upward, dominate the climate and weather of this planet. The downward stream of energy consists of residual solar radiation absorbed by the earth's surface and the atmosphere after about one third is lost by reflection from aerosol clouds and ground. The upward stream is infrared radiation emitted to space by the ground and atmosphere, mostly from atmospheric water vapor, carbon dioxide, and ozone. The albedo (reflectivity of the earth to sunlight) as a whole is 35 percent.

Few surfaces on earth should be dramatically altered for purposes of climate. The deserts might be considered for alteration; their surface has an albedo of 25 to 30 percent. If the albedo is reduced to about 15 percent by a man-made layer of carbon dust over the deserts, the average energy absorbed in the region 40° North to 49° South latitude would be increased by 3.6 calories per square centimeter daily. The average temperature would rise .4°C. However, to lay down so much carbon dust would require half a billion tons of carbon and 50 million sorties by big Air Force Globemasters. A decision to cover the Arctic ice pack and adjacent snow fields would require 1.5 trillion tons of carbon dust and 150 million Globemaster sorties. Such a scheme of climate modification is obviously quite unrealistic.

Another suggestion has been to try seeding and developing ice clouds as screens, thus letting the ice clouds reflect sunlight back into space. Still other proposals would close the Bering Strait and shift the circulation of the Arctic Ocean, thus changing the inland cloud cover and the precipitation and radiation patterns.

What does all this mean in terms of life? We know that ecosystems will adjust to a change in climate, a slow change. We know that stands of vegetation, particular relationships with certain species, will shift northward or southward, depending upon whether there is a warming or a cooling trend. We know that vegetation occupying a continuum changes its association, its relationships, its species along a gradient, and we recognize that if this gradient is changed by weather modification we can expect shifts in the plant and animal population. However, we can be *certain* of only one thing: we know precious little about exactly what changes will occur.

For a number of years we have been trying to understand the coupling between an organism and its immediate climate. We began this task by research with plants for two reasons: plants stand still, and they are easier to work with than animals. Plants have a low metabolic rate compared with many animals, a convenient fact in approaching the subject. We have succeeded in understanding how climate is related to an organism.

But one missing key concept acted as a barrier to proper treatment of this subject: energy. And if you think of climate, you must think of radiation, of wind, of air temperature, of moisture. These are four completely different parameters with different units. Wind is a vector, and temperature is a scalar; you cannot talk about them in the same context. Only through energy can climate really influence an organism and everything that the organism requires. Everything we do—breathing, moving an arm, blinking an eye, sweating—requires energy. If the environment is going to interact with the organism, it is through this flow of energy. Once we understand this simple idea, we can say how the parameters of radiation, wind, air temperature, and moisture can be expressed in terms of energy flow.

To live on this earth, to remain here, we have to be in thermo-dynamic balance. We must be in energy balance. We cannot get more energy than we give out, nor can we get less than we give out. If we get more, we are going to get hotter; if we get less, we are going to get colder. As a steady-state proposition, this is true for every plant and animal on the earth's surface. We spend much of our time in transient states, but generally we have to average out with an energy balance.

These simple notions can help us to understand the relation-ships between climate and an organism. The coupling is through radiation, convection, the flow of air around our surfaces, con-duction if we are in contact with something which is at a differ-ent temperature, evaporation or transpiration or sweating. Of course, metabolism is an energy factor that enters into establish-ing exactly what the relation between a plant or animal and its climatic factors must be in order for the organism to survive.

What makes all of these problems difficult is the fact that, at the very least, we are working with four variables, a four-dimen-sional space. We can understand the two-dimensional space on a graph. We can understand a three-dimensional space conceptually. But when we go to four dimensions or five or six or eight or ten dimensions, as we do with this situation of two or more depend-ent variables and several independent variables, the difficulties multiply. But the problem can be solved.

It is invalid to ask, "What is the effect of air temperature on this plant?" You can only determine the effect of air temperature in the context of a certain amount of radiation, a certain amount of wind, a certain amount of moisture; it depends on all of these factors in simultaneous action.

Let me give you some examples to illustrate the consequences of our climate's impact on us.

If climate and climate change have meaning, they are going to affect the body temperatures of many animals. Normal body temperature is extremely limited for many organisms; if we impose a climate that is going to force it out of that situation, those organisms will be in trouble.

We have to think in terms of limits, as well as of impact. Many organisms begin to deteriorate when their temperatures get above certain points such as 42° or 43°C, which is about 108° or 110°F. In many summertime situations these are not uncommon temperatures for organisms. (Of course, this refers to organism temperature, not air temperature.) Plant leaves get very hot in the summer sun, and often important physiological processes begin to break down because of high temperature. Shift the climate a little bit, get a persistence of hot weather, and trouble appears. There will be a complete change in the plant associations and the ecosystem character. What are some consequences of our calculations? The transpiration rate and leaf temperatures reveal a very interesting series of relations, as do air temperatures and the constant resistance of a plant leaf to water loss. If we identify all the conditions that exist, we can say precisely what a given kind of plant with certain properties will do under any climatic conditions.

Net photosynthesis is a function of temperature; for some plants at approximately 40°C life begins to wane. If the temperature of the plant goes above that, photosynthesis is impaired. Respiration may take over for a while, but after a while it is damaged, too. This is the point: if we have any shift in climate, all the physiological properties of the organism begin to respond and real trouble may follow.

Recently, we tested a theory of which I had been convinced for a long time. I felt that if I knew the properties of an animal I could predict where that creature must live to survive. We have tested this theory on about ten different animals, among them a bird—the cardinal. We examined the relationship between air temperature and radiation absorbed, and then between air temperature and wind speed. We learned that we could forecast exactly when a cardinal had to fly from a sunny treetop and into the shade before being wiped out. We also found that he can endure very cold temperatures in the winter, a fact which has been substantiated in recent years by his migration farther and farther north. We are beginning to understand with precision the relationship between the physiology of the animal—its thermal insulation, its color, its size—and the environment around it. I have great confidence that we are going to find more proof that animals exist within certain environmental limits. They may survive in a smaller niche, but they cannot exist in a larger niche because it would violate their thermodynamic requirements.

How about man himself? We are coupled to the air around us. Near our faces we have a boundary layer across which heat is conducted from the warm skin to the cooler air and across which moisture is lost from the damp skin to the drier air. At the same time, we are breathing or releasing moisture. If air temperature has anything to do with our body temperature—or with the behavior of a plant—it is across this boundary layer. After many experiments, we can say precisely how these interactions take place.

Plants play a dominant role in the determination of climate. The forests, grasslands, shrubs, hedgerows, and shelter belts have an intimate relationship with the climate. All provide protective covering which conserves soil and water, and thus acts to moderate climatic conditions. It seems incredible to me that man has made relatively little effort to understand global weather from the standpoint of the interface between plants and the atmosphere. Another thing on the weather modification problem: we still are working within a domain in which we do not know what we are hazarding. The consequence of introducing some force into the complex system is still only vaguely predictable. We really do not have many of the answers. Some things we do know; and, of course, our knowledge is far broader than it was ten years ago.

The most urgent need is research on the dynamics of the weather and its interaction with animals and particularly plants at the surface. Perhaps, with an understanding of these complex dynamics, we can better discover desperately needed solutions to the problems of modifying climate.

Israel is making great strides in climate modification. It is channeling rainfall into certain basins, into catchment areas for better growth. It is planting trees, which change the weather, making the region more habitable. The same thing is being done in many other parts of the earth.

Do you remember our inadvertent modification of the climate in the midwest dust bowl a few decades ago? We plowed the prairies, a semi-arid region, and we exposed the surface to the elements. The resultant dry period went out of control. Crops would not grow, the grasses would not return. We had dust and devastation. We are not yet secure from such disasters so long as the possibility of inadvertent weather modification hangs over us.

Famine 1975: Fact or Fallacy?

Paul R. Ehrlich

The population problem has already been solved. It took a person willing to step outside the narrow bounds of a discipline, to look at the whole paradigm, to come up with an answer which was both simple and yet unthought of by people working under the strictures of their narrow interests. Dr. Sripati Chandrasekhar, the head of Family Planning in India, came up with the final answer. It will clearly work for India, and it could also work very well in other parts of the world. His proposed solution: at least a one-year moratorium on sexual intercourse in India. However, just in case that does not solve our population and environmental problems, perhaps we should look at them once again so that we will have some background to judge what to do next.

Where did this current crisis come from? Probably, the place to date it is about 8000 years ago when mankind in small groups first gave up a hunting and food-gathering existence and began the practice of agriculture. Two very important things started at that time. First, life became a little more secure. Man was able to produce a more secure food supply and so, slowly but surely, the human death rate (the number of people dying per thousand annually) started to drop. Second, man began to create ecologically unstable situations. He began to arrest succession in early stages to take advantage of the high productivity, and started a process which has continued to this day.

The growth of the human population was slow at first. With a Ouija board, one of the main tools of a demographer, we could

Paul R. Ehrlich is professor of biology and director of graduate study in the Department of Biological Sciences at Stanford University. From his specialty in entomology, he has widened his research into many phases of population biology and evolution. His field work has taken him to many parts of the globe, including the Arctic, Australia, the South Pacific, Southeast Asia, and East Africa.

guess that there were about 5 million people alive around 6000 B.C., and it took until approximately A.D. 1650 to increase that to 500 million. This means that during that 7650-year period the population doubled about every 1000 years. The next doubling required just 200 years; so we had roughly a billion inhabitants of earth around A.D. 1850. In only 80 years, by 1930, mankind numbered 2 billion. Less than 40 years later we are nearing the next doubling; the figure stands at about 3.5 billion. The gap between the death and birth rates is widening so fast that the population of our planet will double in a brief 35 years.

The basic reason for this speed-up is improved socioeconomic conditions which have depressed the death rate. The agricultural revolution came first. Then—particularly between 1500 and 1700 in Europe—improvements in agriculture further lowered the death rate. The succeeding Industrial Revolution did two things: it again bettered people's living conditions and so depressed the death rate, and it started a trend in industrialized countries to lower birth rates slightly.

The medical revolution at the dawn of this century pushed down the death rate even farther, but birth rates in industrial countries were also declining rather rapidly as a result of changed conditions. People no longer looked upon children as a source of farm labor. They could see the possibility of affluence, and children were expensive to educate. So, in the industrialized countries, the birth rate started to follow the death rate down.

With World War II the ultimate castastrophe was upon us in the sense that we took our tremendous medical technology for death control and suddenly disseminated it all over the world. The result: throughout what the euphemists like to call the "undeveloped world" (or, as others more correctly label it, the "hungry world") we had a disastrous decline in the death rate. At the same time there were slight rises in the birth rate, thanks to the eradication of such diseases as gonorrhea in areas where it causes a certain amount of sterility. Thus, by disseminating death control at the end of World War II, we put the finishing touches on our problem so far as the demography goes, and some population growth rates have moved up to degrees which we would have thought theoretically impossible ten or 15 years ago. What we have done is to alter half of the demographic equation, the death rate, without intervening to lower the birth rate.

You can always recognize that someone is kidding you about demography when he talks only in terms of birth rates. You can have a lot of fun saying, "Gee, India has a great program. We are going to reduce the birth rate from 45 to 35 per thousand over the next ten years." This sounds like a big move, because demographers talk classically in terms of numbers per thousand per year instead of percentages. What they do not tell you is that the death rate will simultaneously drop from 14 to 9 per thousand. Therefore, the growth rate, which is the difference between the death and birth rates expressed as a percentage, will remain virtually the same. The clue for discovering whether somebody is pulling your leg when he talks about demography is to find out whether he includes the death rate or talks only about goals in terms of the birth rate.

Our population now is doubling roughly every 35 years. A lot of people ask, "Why can't population grow forever?" The old statistics are still valid for a reply. At the current rate, in 900 years there will be a billion billion people on the face of the earth or 1700 for every square mile. Projecting this farther into the future, in about 2000 or 3000 years people would weigh more than the earth; in 3000 to 4000 years, the mass of humans would equal the size of a sphere with the same diameter as the earth's orbit around the sun; in 5000 years everything in the visible universe would be converted into people, and their expansion would be at the speed of light. All of those mathematically foreseeable results are far enough in the future to relieve us of any necessity for worry.

Occasionally, someone can be convinced that population growth will end sooner or later. Unfortunately for us, it is going to be sooner, because like other organisms with a very rapid population increase, we tend to press on our resources, and the second part of the population-food environment crisis is that we are running out of food. Out of the 3.5 billion humans on earth today, between 1 and 2 billion are malnourished or under-nourished.

The number who are actually starving is a matter for some debate, since we have the problem of how to define starvation. It is very difficult to starve someone to death. He has to live in an abiotic environment with a slow deprivation of food. Otherwise, he will be carried away by pneumonia, the flu, or something else before he even technically gets a chance to starve to death.

Demographic statistics produced by most countries arise from imagination. The Indians, for instance, just make up their figures. The ones that might be valid are created in curious ways. In the *New York Times Magazine* of October 13, 1968, correspondent Joseph Lelyveld in India had the following commentary which sums it up very well: "The Indian government does not like to concede that there is starvation in the country and so splits hairs by insisting that all grossly undernourished persons who die are actually carried off by identifiable diseases, thereby side-stepping the fact that it is precisely the lack of food that makes killers of what would otherwise be curable ailments."

If we take the only intelligent definition of starvation—that a person is starved to death if an adequate diet would have assured survival—then the level of deaths due to starvation in the world today is truly colossal, somewhere between 5 million and 20 million people a year. Again, we have this definition problem. The statistics are worse where the problem is worse, but there is a tremendous amount of death from starvation. It is estimated that of 530 million Indians, only 10 million have an adequate diet. This reveals a lot, also, about the sluggishness, the laziness, of tropical peoples; a great many characteristics that we regard as natural sloth result from combined malnutrition and high levels of parasite infection. A recent series of studies has shown, for instance, that a person with a low protein diet early in life finds it virtually impossible ever to catch up, so far as IQ or brain volume is concerned, to say nothing of physical size.

Evolutionarily, from an anthropomorphic view, we faced a little problem a good number of millions of years ago: How do you have a child with a very big head and, at the same time, women who are not shaped entirely like bells? Somehow, you must get that head out through the mother's pelvis at birth. Evolution solved it by providing for the majority of brain growth immediately after birth. Of course, brain growth involves protein synthesis; you synthesize proteins from components of other proteins that you have digested. If either the mother in the late stages of pregnancy or the child early in life does not have an adequate diet, the youngster never catches up and becomes a mentally retarded individual.

Many of the reasons for our own starvation and poverty problems in this country can be traced to the Department of Agriculture's running of our food programs and feeding white flour and lard to people who are on relief, rather than having the Department of Health, Education, and Welfare do it and feed adequate protein-rich food to the disadvantaged.

An extremely serious starvation problem exists on earth at this moment. In 1965 and 1966 a tremendous crisis in world agriculture was blamed on "bad weather." It was a "good" year in 1967; there was a 3 percent worldwide rise in agricultural productivity. However, it was an increase from the low 1965-66 base, and in 1967 per capita food production (which is the critical thing) had not caught up to 1964. So things were very bad. They continue to be very bad.

Summing up so far, we have too many people and a ridiculously high growth rate, and we are running out of food.

Several other things have not been pointed out often in the area of population growth. First, all demographic projections are linear. This does not mean they are necessarily straight lines. They may be curvilinear, but when you hear a prediction that we are going to have 7 billion or 7.5 billion people in the year 2000, it is based on the assumption that you can continue the curve.

However, there are some very fancy possibilities for discontinuities caused by increasing death rates. Famine is only one possible death-rate solution if we are not careful. Thermonuclear war is rather obvious to everybody. Interestingly enough, a top science adviser of the British government quite willingly has acknowledged to me that population pressures are, and will continue to be, adding to political tension and instability; but he was not willing to admit that population pressures would therefore add to the possibility of thermonuclear war. I leave the question open for evaluation; I am no expert in this field.

The potential for worldwide pestilence has been neglected by people interested in the population-food crisis. At this moment we have the largest population of human beings that has ever lived on the Earth. There are now more hungry and weakened people on this planet than there were human beings in 1850. We have jet airplanes capable of carrying sick people around the globe in about 24 hours. We know that viruses have a tendency to do crazy things when they circulate in large populations, so there is always a possibility of a virus giving us a super influenza. This could end the population explosion abruptly.

We know, too, that biological warfare laboratories are cooking up all sorts of nightmarish "weapons." (I am told that it is theoretically possible to develop a virus against which there is absolutely no resistance.) They are trying to breed drug-resistant strains of anthrax, and I am sure that they are having quite a lot of success. There have been rumblings about rabies in a pneumonic form. Rabies can be transmitted as an aerosol under very special conditions—in bat caves, for instance—and it is not a tremendous stretch of the imagination to think that a pneumonic rabies could be created. We have been assured that biological laboratories are escape-proof, that nothing will ever get out, any more than nerve gas would ever get loose because conditions there are absolutely safe, or than an underground atomic test would ever vent because the Atomic Energy Commission assures us of its impossibility. Curiously enough, though, men like Joshua Lederberg and Sir Macfarlane Burnet (both Nobel laureates in medicine and physiology) are a bit nervous about how escape-proof biological warfare labs are. Apparently here is another possibility for a discontinuity to end the population explosion by sharply bringing up the death rate again.

The third part of the equation is environmental deterioration. Anybody who has eyes or a nose should be well aware of it. There are several points to be made about environmental deterioration: we are changing the climate of the earth in various ways, by the pollutants we put into the atmosphere, by deforestation, and so on. Changing the climate cuts down agricultural productivity because people are extremely conservative in their agricultural practices. Once we have modified the weather, we have to plant different crops; a transition to a new kind of crop culture means a depression in the amount of food, so that kind of environmental deterioration plays directly back on our food supply. A very serious and desperate moral problem follows as a result of our frantic attempts to create more and more food.

A politically active petrochemical industry has created in this country preposterous pesticide procedures in which everybody is persuaded to spray on schedule whether there are pests present or not. K. E. F. Watt of the University of California (Davis) has done a lot of systems analyses on this problem; his general conclusion seems to be that pesticide usage in the United States is a losing game financially for everyone except the petrochemical industry.

Biologists have long been able to tell people that broadcast usage of pesticides is ecologically ignorant. Thanks to the second law of thermodynamics and other considerations, herbivore populations are virtually always larger than predator populations; they automatically contain a greater degree of genetic variability, and therefore they are most likely to become genetically resistant. I would also point out something of which most people in the pesticide business do not seem to be aware: plants have been in the pesticide business longer than industrialists; virtually all plant biochemicals are antibiotic agents of one kind or another, mostly aimed at insects. The insects have been evolving in this system for a long time; they have already prepared themselves to be poisoned and are quite capable of developing resistance. Despite many professional conversations, I have yet to hear of a single case where a pest insect has been eradicated through pesticide usage, although there are many cases of nonpest insects winning promotion to pest status by ridiculous pesticide usage. So the whole thing—how pesticides are applied, how extremely resistant pests are to change, and how ignorant people are of this entire problem—really beggars the imagination.

Pesticides recently have been shown to reduce photosynthesis in marine phytoplankton. We know there is plenty of DDT in the ocean because it shows up in rather high quantities in Antarctic seals, Antarctic penguins, and other organisms not subjected to daily spraying. There is now rather strong evidence that chlorinated hydrocarbon poisoning may already be a major cause of human mortality, and that the worst is yet to come.

We have an extremely serious problem in the way agriculturists think about agricultural revolution. Producing more food almost always involves dramatic deterioration of the environment. In fact, it usually involves the worst possible consequence: simplifying the ecosystem.

Basically then, we have a tripartite problem. We have too many people and an incredible growth rate, and we are just about out of food. And we have this fantastically difficult and important problem of environmental deterioration; this scares me much more than being almost out of food, because we are quite capable of turning off the life-support systems on which we absolutely depend.

Why isn't something being done? One of the best reasons is that there are a great many people, narrowly trained technologists, who can see only their own little areas. They keep publishing absolutely absurd things about how we are going to save the world with this, that, or the other simple solution.

At a population meeting in Princeton some time ago, a suggested cure was to look into ways of shipping our surplus population to the other planets. The person who proposed this is a typical technological optimist; he can do anything but count. Let me make a few optimistic assumptions. Let's suppose that an Apollo spacecraft could carry 100 people. That would require some modifications; it would be a bit crowded, but let's do it—100 colonists. Let's assume that it could not just put people into orbit but could carry them to any planet. Let's assume that the uninhabitable planets of our solar system were really inhabitable. And let's assume that you could send off these rocket ships for exactly the same cost as an Apollo craft, even though they would have to be much larger, more complex, and there would be the extra cost of rounding up and training all the colonists.

We *could* keep the population of the earth constant in number by exporting surplus humans. All we would have to do is send off 2000 of our normal-sized Apollo space vessels every day. The daily cost would be $300 billion. That is the equivalent of our Gross National Product in less than three days, so we really would have to pay hefty taxes to get such a job done.

If we could get Congress to repeal the laws of thermodynamics and a few other things, it would take only 250 years at the present growth rate for humans to occupy the entire solar system to exactly the present population density of the earth. If we then wanted to move on to the stars, which involves some slightly bigger logistical problems (we do not want to get into them because we are being optimists) we would face the fact that the nearest stars with possible habitable planets are a long way off. They would take generations to reach. We would have to export people willing to practice strict birth control, and leave the technological optimists and other people back here to breed. That would be quite a program!

Actually, such thinking does a lot of damage. We all can laugh at it because *we* presumably know that doing something with 70 million more people a year—and that is the yearly increment (more than the population of the United States every three years)—is not so easily solved. But every time someone appropriately "reputable" says, "When it gets really tough here, we will send our surplus to the stars," he gets newspaper headlines; and everyone says, "Well, that is a solution to the problem. We can forget about it. Turn on the pollution, George. They are going to take care of everything, and there is no problem."

The AEC has been in this game recently. It did a huge feasibility study for feeding the underdeveloped world. (Let's hope that part of the globe stays underdeveloped, because if we ever tried to develop it, the world would end for reasons I will explain later.)

The AEC came up with a few simple technological assumptions. For instance, it is going to be able to develop functional breeder reactors. That is not too bad an idea, although it may overestimate the speed at which we will get them. After a lot of figuring it found that it could build nuclear agro-industrial complexes on the seashore in which nuclear power could desalt water. It reached more optimistic assumptions about the cost of desalted water than any expert in desalinization would make, but we will give it that; we are going to give it all its assumptions. Then, it would create fertilizer and make a wonderful complex capable of feeding 3 million people.

This can be done for a mere $1.5 billion per complex. So far as I can find out, that estimate does not include the cost of buying the land, or shipping people to the food or food to the people if the complex is put in an uninhabited area, or training the technicians, or maintenance, or anything like that. But let's just use the $1.5 billion figure as the total cost. If the AEC began this project tomorrow and could finish it within a decade, we would have to put in $400 billion (a very large sum when you recall that our annual foreign aid is $2 billion) simply to feed the 770 million people who will be added to the population during those ten years. Assuming all the AEC assumptions are correct, the 1978-88 decade would cost about $500 billion and the 1988-98 decade about $600 billion, which means that we would have spent somewhere around $1500 billion by 1998.

At that point, we would be worse off than today. All the people who are hungry today still would be hungry then. We would not have fed any of them, just the increase.

We would have all the environmental deterioration associated with this fantastic complex: all the pesticides that would have been dumped, all the salt which nobody would know what to do with. If you dump the salt back into the ocean as brine, you kill off the inshore richness of the sea, which is one of the places where you can get some food; if you leave it lying out in huge pans, it blows into the sky and changes the weather.

Here are serious people who have put together this absolutely preposterous scheme. The way they set it up, we could not even start to build one of these nuclear agro-industrial complexes with the equivalent of our present foreign aid funds—not one. Yet we would need hundreds of them just to cope with the population increase alone. Let's suppose that people were willing to spend just the first ten years' $400 billion. With that much money we could offer $650 bounties for vasectomies to 500 million young men. We even could set aside $100 for the medical costs of doing each vasectomy. That is a tremendous input of money, but let me point out that $650 equals eight years' income for the average Indian. They are trying to sell vasectomies in India for a couple of dollars apiece or a cheap transistor radio. The difference of scale is tremendous, and if we could get even a sizable portion of the males to accept such a tremendous bounty, we would instantly solve a very large part of the essential population problem. This, of course, hinges on whether or not we want to spend that kind of money.

Technological optimists have other schemes for feeding the world that are not quite so far out. They include the "unmeasurable" resources of the sea which have really been measured very accurately and found to be wanting. By now it is quite commonly recognized that most of the sea is a biological desert, very unproductive. Most of the productivity is inshore where we are now facing colossal pollution problems around the globe. Thermodynamically, what we do at sea anyway is equivalent to harvesting lions on land, using only the top of the food chain.

Besides the tremendous problem of ocean pollution, we can see now the beginning of what is probably world history's biggest race. That is the race to loot the sea of what protein it still contains. The Japanese, the Russians, the Chileans, the Americans, the Norwegians, and many others are building huge, more efficient fleets to sail out and get what there is while the getting is good. For instance, an undeclared shooting war exists between Mexico and Japan off Baja California because of Japanese fishing-fleet activities. The northern countries are moving into southern waters because their own seas have become depleted. A single Rumanian ship with "space-age" equipment recently outfished all 1500 ships of the New Zealand fleet.

The oceans will never be a tremendously important source of calories, although they might continue to supply a significant amount of animal protein. If we have the agricultural revolution in the tropics with pesticides, as some undeveloped countries now plan, very soon they will not be any source of food at all.

Another scheme involves growing microorganisms on algae or the fecal slime of sewage treatment plants. It is not clear to me who is going to eat this stuff, but that is one of the proposals I have recently picked up in a newspaper story. It is of some consequence to note that the hungry people in the world are much more conservative about their food habits than we are. Why? Because to them food is a very limited number of items. We have trouble, for instance, convincing some people to eat IR-8 rice (this is the new high-yield rice grain developed in the Philippines at the International Rice Research Institute); they balk if it is too starchy and sticks together, since they are used to eating rice that falls apart. People will starve to death in rice areas rather than eat wheat, which they do not recognize as food. And yet somebody suggests taking algae from the sewage treatment plants and shipping it overseas to feed the hungry! Imagine the propaganda aspects of this particular plan. Fortunately, nobody is really trying to push it. We can grow microorganisms on petroleum and get protein, quite true. Nobody has tried to market it. Attempts have been made to market food additives such as Incaparina (corn combined with high-protein cotton-seed meal, Vitamin A, and yeast, developed by the Nutrition Institute of Central America and Panama), which is quite close to what we regard as food. But in Latin America for about the last 15 years efforts to get people to use this as a food supplement have been a total failure.

Recently I saw in a popular periodical a plan for farming blue whales in coral atolls; it was a real beauty, and I will not bother to describe it. The direct synthesis of food is put forth as a possible solution by people who do not understand thermodynamics. One little old lady asked me, "Can't we all eat dehydrated food like the astronauts?"

All of the technological panaceas for increasing food production are either impractical, impossible, ludicrous, or worse. One that is highly touted by our Department of Agrobusiness in Washington is known in the trade as the "Green Revolution." I believe the "Revolution" is to be created in the bankrolls of certain businesses in the United States, because it certainly is not being created anywhere else. The reversal of stories from the U.S. Department of Agriculture is something magnificent to behold. In the 1965-66 "bad weather" time, everybody was filled with pessimism. Then, in 1967, the weather improved in India and the other key regions. All of a sudden agriculture was doing a great job; all the high-yield wheat, sorghum, and rice varieties were going to save the world. This is still the current story.

If we are going to increase food production, the most intelligent way is to get higher yields from land already in cultivation. There is nothing wrong with that idea if it is done with great care for the ecological consequences—which, of course, it is not. But there are all kinds of problems in the new high-yield grains; they are high-yield only with proper cultivation, including a great input of fertilizer, and in most of the areas where they are being planted, there are serious problems of fertilizer distribution. Raymond H. Ewell at the State University of New York (Buffalo) has been India's chief fertilizer consultant for the last dozen years; he says quite frankly that he does not think that India has a hope of producing enough. It is certainly impossible for the United States to produce enough fertilizer for India, in addition to meeting our domestic needs, to get the maximum yield out of these grains; it also seems unlikely that the world will donate enough fertilizer to India. So there is a very big fertilizer problem. You have to grow crops exactly right to get successful harvests. From what other people and I have seen personally in India, the chance of their doing things exactly right seems to be about zero. An even more serious problem arises in planting grains which have been inadequately field tested against pest and blight resistance because this project is rush-rush. Already IR-8 rices have had a lot of trouble from this problem (recently "miracle rats" have invaded "miracle rice" fields in the Phillippines), but even bigger monocultures are being created. A complete switch to the new high-yield grain varieties would leave India with only about half of the possible diversity of wheat strains. This means that, instead of a Bihar or a Pakistan famine, when a virus gets in and wipes out the crops, it will cover a much larger area. These are dangers of increased monoculture.

Another problem which seems to be endemic to agriculturists is that almost all of their projections are based on optimism—that good years are normal years. When I visited Australia, that country was having a colossal drought, and the agriculturists were saying in the press: "This is once in a million years; we have got to build, we have got to get relief; everything is going to be all right when the rains come." However, Australian weather records indicate that similar droughts occur with monotonous regularity every ten years or so. It is the same story in India, the same in China. They have deforested most of their land; among other things, this helps to create unstable weather. We know very well that you cannot expect long stretches of good years. There are good years interspersed with doses of bad years. For instance, last July the Indian government—which was churning out all kinds of propaganda about how it is going to become self-sufficient in agriculture by 1971—was so pleased with the year's crops that it created a special commemorative postage stamp about the great agricultural breakthrough. If India, which now can feed adequately only 10 million out of 530 million inhabitants, is to gain self-sufficiency in food by 1971, it will mean feeding 530 million people—plus an increment of 50 to 60 million. I have yet to meet any person who has been there who thinks that India could possibly be close to self-sufficiency in food by 1971. Indeed, I am willing to predict that India will never be self-sufficient in food unless it succeeds in cutting its population far back.

The headlines of the "Green Revolution" have been seen all over India. The Indian government is afraid that we will not send them any more food if it does not make progress in agriculture, so it makes unwarranted claims. However, if you look in the *New York Times*, you will find the following pieces of information: on September 24, 1968, six of 17 Indian states were drought-stricken, with uncertain crop outlooks; the Indian government was looking around for additional food; on October 13, a cholera epidemic hit other states of India which were flooded.

Still, agriculturists have a general feeling that somehow these new crops will solve the world's food problem. This feeling resulted primarily from a square yard of corn planted in Iowa. Five agronomists crouched over it constantly, gave it absolutely perfect everything, and got a yield from it. Then they ran inside, took out an atlas, and figured how many square yards there are in the Amazon basin. By multiplication they determined the amount of food that could be provided in the Amazon basin—and everything is going to be all right.

Unfortunately, that just is not the way the game is played. We do not know how to farm the tropics. We do know that most tropical soils are abysmal. We are not really making substantial progress with farming anywhere in the tropics, and it seems highly unlikely that we are going to. In other words, we will score some little gains with these high-yield crops, but they will be made at great ecological risk.

Here is another quotation, this one from a *Time* book review:

> The neo-Malthusians want to warn man of danger, but their alarm is so loud that it may have the effect of deafening the world to its opportunities. To the real agricultural scientists close to the soil and its sciences, such pessimism sounds silly or worse. They are sure that the modern world has both soil and the scientific knowledge to feed, and feed well, twice as many people as are living today. By the time the population has increased that much man may, and probably will have, discovered new ways of increasing his food supply.

The article describes the optimism of a Dr. R. Salter of —guess what!—the U.S. Department of Agrobusiness about how we can feed the 2.25 billion humans who the Food and Agriculture Organization (FAO) of the United Nations predicted would be living in 1960. The quotation is from *Time* of November 8, 1948. Actually, when 1960 arrived, there were 3 billion people living, not the 2.25 billion estimated by the FAO. (*Time*, by the way, thought the 2.25 billion was probably a high estimate.) It is also a fact that in 1960 those agriculture experts were not adequately feeding even 2 billion of the 3 billion.

I wish I could avoid taking some of the blame for the agricultural experts, but academic biologists have a large share here. In my generation we were trained to think that anything pertaining to agriculture or applied or technical study was dirty, not to be mentioned, and we had to go into esoteric research. As a result, we have produced a generation of agriculturists who can farm Iowa beautifully; they can get out press releases beautifully, but they cannot count and do not realize what the world situation is. We have a generation of agriculturists who, I am afraid, do not realize what really dreadful results their propaganda is having. My story for them still must be the same; I have told it to a good number of them. They stand up in meetings and say, "But, you know we can do high-yield this and high-yield that." I reply, "When you can feed the 3.5 billion people living today, come around again, and we will talk about going on to 7 billion. Until then, sit down and shut up, because you are not doing any good."

The summary is very simple. We have dramatically outstripped our food supply with our population growth, and we are destroying our planet. The title of my discussion here is supposed to be "Famine 1975: Fact or Fallacy?" I do not know whether we are going to have famine in 1975 in the context it is usually put. We have famine right now over most of the earth, if you want to define famine as people being hungry. We have famine right now over most of the earth, if you want to define it as people starving to death. You might want to define it as that level of famine at which every American will become aware of it, because there will be almost nothing else in the newspapers. The timing of such a massive famine will depend on just a couple of things. (This is, of course, skipping the possible discontinuity—a thermonuclear war or a massive plague—either or both of which could help us avoid famine.) It will depend slightly on how successful the agriculturists are in increasing food yields, because that will put the famine off in time and make the crash bigger when it comes. And it will depend very largely on the weather. I think an estimate of 1975 is still as good as we can make, but it could be anywhere from 1972 to 1985, depending primarily on luck. I think the actual date is a quibble.

What can we do about all this? Do we just sit back and let the whole food supply system go down the drain as it is now, or do we try to do something? Those are difficult questions. If we are going to do something, we must first get the situation in the United States under some kind of control. This country needs fewer inhabitants. We must stop our population growth; we must get our population down to a size which we can properly maintain, and we have to do all kinds of dramatic things to save what is left of our environment.

In this country the rich are getting richer, the poor are getting poorer; among the nations of the earth the same situation holds true. Nobody trusts our motives. The white majority in our country must convince Black Power advocates that there is no effective conspiracy to wipe out the blacks through population control. It is quite clear that a lot of people who advocate population control really mean to stop the blacks from breeding, but that is a typically inept viewpoint that you would expect of a racist. Actually, nothing could be better for the black community than to avoid the problem of black mothers with eight or nine children who do not get proper care and who do not have proper fatherly guidance. It is quite clear that in the world today group numbers mean nothing. It is the *quality* of people that matters. So if the racists are really trying to get to the blacks by promoting population control among them, then the racists are working to defeat their own ends.

We have similar problems in other countries. Former President Arthur da Costa e Silva of Brazil recently said that population control is decadent and that more people are needed to develop South America. He governed one of the few countries in South America that has a prayer of hope for bettering the lives of its people. But if his successors retain such opinions and act on them, they will guarantee that the prayer is unanswered.

First we must get things under control in the United States, and this involves some complicated maneuvering to overcome a great many difficulties. It will involve governmental intervention, changes in tax structure, and formidable changes in attitude. I believe we can get the job done in this country without real governmental coercion. However, when you start looking at other nations, the problems escalate monstrously because they do not have equivalent communications systems and we do not understand enough about their cultural fabric. We understand enough to know that family planning does not work, that just making available condoms, intrauterine devices (IUDs) and contraceptive pills does not work. The basic problem lies in the people's attitudes, particularly toward family size. We must find a much greater variety of approaches—economic and governmental—which probably will be different in every country and require colossal, simultaneous campaigns. We hope each will work, and we will have to find out quickly why they do not work if they show signs of failure. It is going to be fantastically difficult. We will need worldwide and governmental policy planning of an unfamiliar type. We will have to figure out where our aid can be spent best, rather than scatter it indiscriminately. We will have to recognize the fact that most countries can never industrialize and that giving them industrialization aid is wasteful. We will have to accept the fact (already shown by theory, computer simulation, and practice) that it is pointless to help any country with a rapidly growing population unless the aid is very largely for population control, or at least unless such population control aid is included.

We are going to have to make so many changes in our behavior pattern and in the minds of men that I frankly tend toward tremendous pessimism. People say to me, "What do you think our chances are?" I answer that our chances for success may be 2 percent now, and that if we work really hard, we might move them up to 3 percent.

A great deal of political action is needed first and foremost in this country. If you do not want to be bothered with this sort of thing, perhaps you can adopt a philosophy which I find rather appealing: if you book passage on the *Titanic*, there is no point in going steerage.

The Harvest of the Seas:
How Fruitful and for Whom?

Georg Borgstrom

One phase of the world food issue is increasingly becoming the focus of attention. This is the role of the ocean, and it, more than any other area, is subject to a great deal of misinterpretation.

As a preface, take note of the overall situation today. We are faced with a backlog of no fewer than 2.5 billion people in the world who are short of almost everything, particularly food and water. In terms of food, the protein shortage is most evident. We are in an unprecedented population explosion, adding a number of people each year which is equivalent to the population of three Canadas or, if you prefer, a new United States each third year. This means that in terms of the next ten years we have to find food for no fewer than 1000 million more people.

During the post-World War II period we lost at least 20 precious years by accepting the notion that this whole issue was merely a question of producing more food. We believed what the agriculturists and other technologists were assuring the human race, that we had the technology to provide food for almost any number of people. As documented through the technical assistance programs, our accomplishments under this idea were unique. Through this mobilization of a global technical Salvation Army, we operated extremely successfully. In the history of agriculture there has never been a period when such tremendous gains were made.

Georg Borgstrom is professor of food science and economic geography at Michigan State University, East Lansing. He is an authority on world food resources and their utilization, as well as on the balance between population and resources. He has published several major books, particularly on the role of trade and fisheries in global feeding, and the earth's food situation. Besides being a member of many scientific and professional scientific organizations, he is a fellow of the 300-member World Academy of Arts and Sciences.

Nevertheless, we failed. When the United Nations' Food and Agriculture Organization (FAO) held its twentieth anniversary, it could only look at the degree of failure beside the tremendous successes. The successes were not sufficient to cope with the growth of the human race. We had more hungry, starving, and malnourished individuals than ever before in human history. Furthermore, the situation had become chronic.

At that time, about five years ago, the international organizations recognized the problem and put the population issue on the books. Their approach was two-dimensional: more food and fewer people. I submit that we failed to recognize several other dimensions such as those of food spoilage and utilization, nutritional needs, and disease patterns. On the whole, an understanding of the supreme biological (ecological) dimension has all the time been woefully lacking. The medical profession's newfound therapeuticals may enable man to live longer. But it is not sufficient to have people simply surviving; they must be provided with food.

You have undoubtedly read about the oceans being an almost limitless source of protein, a reserve of food for almost any number of people. Look at what has happened on the marine scene. With a certain pride, the fisheries people have pointed to the fact that world fisheries—in contrast to world agriculture—have been able to match the growth of the human race with their increase in catches. There has hardly ever been a period in the history of mankind in which so much emphasis has been put on the development of world fisheries. Never in the history of world fisheries have such tremendous gains been made as in the postwar period. We have more than tripled the catches, and we have provided for large new modern fleets operating in almost all waters. Hardly any major fishing grounds remain that are not visited by fishing fleets.

For example, consider the Falkland Shelf off Argentina. Because she is well provided with protein through her meat, Argentina has not paid much attention to her fisheries and has done little to tap the rich protein resources off her coast. A recent look at the facts showed, however, that fleets from many nations are now operating on this shelf: the Soviet Union, Japan, East and West Germany, Poland, Spain, Israel, as well as several others. In other words, the shelf is swarming with catching fleets.

This is a period of revolutionary upheaval in world fisheries. First, the big new fleets are provided with super-modern electronic devices, with new gear, and with new materials superior to anything they ever had in the past. Second, to a much greater degree than ever before, the catching fleets are provided with processing facilities such as refrigerated holds, and freezing, salting, and drying facilities.

In addition to these two developments, several floating factories have been launched and brought into operation with lines for manufacture of frozen, canned, and salted items. Waste is converted into meal and oil. Transport vessels, search vessels, and many other specialized units operate with these mother ships. Indeed, it is no exaggeration to refer to this as a revolutionary period within fisheries.

Four features most vividly describe what has been happening. The first is the resurgence of Japan as a top-ranking fishing nation, a position she held in the 1930s. During that period, to a small degree, the Japanese started the development of floating factories with the establishment of their salmon-canning factories in the North Pacific.

This rebuilding of Japanese fishing started after 1952, when the U.S. occupation formally terminated. But in the rich waters on the inside of the homeland Japan faced severe limitations in the form of restriction lines drawn by Mao Tse-tung, Nikolai Bulganin, and Syngman Rhee. The so-called Bulganin Line, for instance, cut off the Sea of Okhotsk, where Japan used to do a great deal of fishing. All these restrictions were implemented and enforced, which meant that any Japanese ship violating the lines was immediately seized and held. Some were returned only after long-time restraint and protracted negotiations.

Japan was forced to move out into the entire Pacific. This was nothing new in Japanese history, because Japan actually had developed fisheries in the whole Far East area of Czarist Russia. There were many Japanese fishing colonies even up Siberian rivers on the Arctic flank. Back in the nineteenth century Japan had already developed fisheries on and off Sakhalin and retained her sovereignty over the southern part of Sakhalin (Karafuto) right up to her defeat in World War II. She also developed canneries and salting establishments. Because she was such a populous nation compared with the vast, sparsely populated Czarist region, Japan was the chief market for a great deal of the Russian catches. Of course, as the Soviet regime came in, it gradually pushed out the Japanese from area after area. Finally, the Japanese only held on to southern Sakhalin.

After World War II, the Japanese went out over the Pacific to the islands where they had operated prior to the conflict. I have always wondered what Commodore Perry would have said, had he known what was to emerge from his opening-up gambit. He praised God when he had signed the agreement of access to Japan in 1854. What would he have thought if he could see that three generations later the population explosion has tripled the numbers and pushed that country 8000 miles north and south and 8000 miles east and west! It is something to ponder.

In fisheries, Japan did not limit herself to a Pacific expansion. She went into the Indian Ocean, into the Atlantic, and she even joined the North Atlantic fisheries. The Mediterranean is largely dominated by Japanese fishing, and approximately 11 bases in the Caribbean area are Japanese.

The characteristic feature of this large-scale operation is that it is founded on an arrangement of local operational bases. This means the Japanese secured land areas where they built storage and freezing houses as a temporary arrangement. From these local bases, they can pick up the catches at their convenience, and take them back to Japan. In other instances Japanese operations are based on joint companies in respective countries. Virtually every nation in the Mediterranean has an international Japanese fishing company. Most of the ships are Japanese, but they are registered under the flags of Yugoslavia, Greece, Italy, etc. The Japanese have even created a Japanese-Israeli company, as well as a Japanese-Egyptian company. They broke or deviated from this type of pattern only in the North Pacific area where they pursued their earlier efforts of catching and canning salmon at sea, and later expanded into crab.

In the 1930s Japan had supremacy in the North Pacific. Today the USSR has taken over this position. Japan has to negotiate catch quotas with the USSR for salmon and crab every year. About 15 Japanese floating factories used to operate in the Sea of Okhotsk. In the postwar period Japan has been permitted at the most, one unit a year, except one year when it was allowed two units.

During a sojourn in Japan, I visited a big canning factory and saw workers packing bonito, sometimes called skipjack. I asked the proprietor where the skipjack came from. It is an old Japanese fish and very important to the poor of Japan. I was told that it was caught in Japanese waters. Later, I found out that this skipjack was actually caught in the Middle Atlantic and taken to the Canary Islands, which for all practical purposes have become Japanese. (The main traffic in the Canaries is due to Japanese fishing. Similar arrangements were later made with the Portuguese as regards the Azores.) That skipjack was frozen on the Canaries, transported by Swedish freighter to Yokohama, and then stored at the factory until needed.

The fish was put in beautiful, lithographed, colored cans with English text. I was told it was intended for the homeland market. As a result of the American occupation, they explained, Japan is extremely fond of the English language. On the back of the can there was a brief Japanese text. My skepticism finally brought out the truth: some of these cans went to Malaya for the Europeans living there; about one third of this pack was sold to Italy; the scrapings were put in nonlithographed cans for sale on the Japanese market.

This brings me to the essential point: the overwhelming bulk of the long-distance catches go back to Japan. The tuna catches are only partly returned home. Most enter the world market. The bases in the Caribbean are really providing the big U.S. canneries in Puerto Rico with tuna. Japan is also selling a great deal of tuna to California. This tuna either arrives unprepared or frozen in cans with loose lids. This reduces customs duties. In California the cans are sealed and processed.

The Japanese crab is put on the world market under the Geisha label, as is the corresponding Russian crab under the Chatka label. Only a fraction of the Japanese catch goes to Japan. High-grade canned salmon is being sold to England. These are the major limitations on what is being brought to Japan.

A walk through the Tokyo fish market is a most remarkable zoological adventure, as well as a geographic venture. Big blackboards indicate from which fishing grounds the fish lots originate; they show catches from all parts of the Pacific Ocean, from the Indian Ocean, and from all major regions of the Atlantic. The majority of the catches are brought in frozen, then defrosted and sold on the fresh market of Tokyo. (Some nonprocessed fish in our own country is actually sold under these same conditions.)

The annual catch of Japan is now up to about 7 million metric tons. There was a brief stagnation in the beginning of the 1960s, mainly due to overfishing in the Middle Atlantic. The fleets were forced to relocate in new grounds. Some were moved back to better yielding waters in the Indian Ocean.

The second feature to focus attention on is the massive ocean invasion by the Soviet land giant. This is in many ways a more remarkable venture than the Japanese resurgence, particularly in two ways: One, Czarist Russia did not have the maritime tradition of Japan; the Soviets had to create that. This meant that they had to establish training schools for navigation and for fishing. Several research centers for fisheries were started, etc. Much was needed for such a tremendous expansion: the creation of an equipment industry, oceanographic surveys, and biological appraisal of fishery resources.

The other thing that makes the Soviet endeavor particularly remarkable relates to the political sphere. The USSR could not follow the Japanese pattern. It had to be independent of regional support. This is why it was forced to move its processing facilities—some involving final stages—out to sea and operate them on the fishing grounds. For this purpose the Soviets created a whole fleet of modernly equipped processing units (so-called mother ships) with facilities to manufacture canned, frozen, dried, and salted fish, and with equipment for complete utilization of all waste by its conversion into meal, saving oil, vitamins, etc. Incidentally, it is forbidden on Soviet ships to throw anything overboard.

Soviet publications, even as far back as the 1930s, show that a great deal of experimentation was then conducted on a full scale by the building and testing of vessels equipped for freezing, salting, and other necessary processing steps. These ships were actually sent out to sea and studied, not merely in terms of one or another detail, but in terms of the total operation from catch to final product. It is no easy task to move processing facilities from land-based conditions onto a ship which may be hit in a gale or where space is extremely limited. There was a pressing need for intensive investigation to find the optimum use of space, to reduce the space required for various equipment, and to learn how to make such equipment operate effectively even under severe weather conditions. This transfer was an impressive undertaking, and it seems that it has been notably successful. Full advantage was also taken of early European and American experiments with freezing trawlers.

Another aspect is the fact that not all the Soviet ships were built in the USSR. The first ones were placed on order in West Germany after World War II. Still today the USSR has, by my estimation, between 50 and 80 units on order with shipyards outside of the Soviet Union.

The first such specialized units built after World War II were freezing trawlers, ordered from West German shipyards and called Pushkins. Each was about 2400 gross registered tons, and it started out with an operational efficiency of about 6000 tons of fish a year. Today, most of them are exceeding 10,000 tons. In other words, they have almost doubled their capacity. Transporting vessels have been added to carry back the catches, thus making it superfluous for the processing units to make lengthy return journeys. Some crews are substituted by helicopter from servicing ships.

An important feature to remember is that the Soviet activities, like the Japanese, expand to almost all waters in the Pacific, the Atlantic, the Indian Ocean, and the Antarctic. To put it in their terms and in the organizational terms I have been describing, it really means that each Soviet fleet is a working city—and I do mean exactly that, because it does hard work, employing about 25,000 to 30,000 men.

The North Atlantic fleets go out from Murmansk, which is ice-free most of the year, although it is on the Arctic front. Murmansk became familiar to many beleaguered seamen during World War II when it was one of the chief doorways through which the Allies brought support to the USSR. This once simple seaport is now the largest fishing port on earth in terms of human food.

An interesting Soviet book recently maintained that through Murmansk have passed 15 million metric tons of fish (up to 1967), half of that in the last ten years. The figure registered for 1967 was 890,000 tons, which means almost 2 billion pounds. This is a good way of putting into perspective what the Soviets are doing, because they hope to expand considerably the present annual catch—about 5.6 million metric tons and climbing very rapidly—to reach 10 million metric tons in 1972. It is my opinion that they will reach this figure, because of the extent to which they are expanding their fleet and their operations. If you put it in terms of Murmansk, they are counting on bringing in 4 billion pounds in 1980 to that one port. This shows the impetus of their development and also their grand design.

Parenthetically, the USSR has a similar big drive on in terms of a merchant navy. The big question in naval circles is whether by 1972 the Soviet Union will not have the largest merchant navy in the world, surpassing any other in numbers of units and efficiency. So this marine expansion is not limited to the area of fishing.

The figures in the Soviet development plans indicate that the catch in the Far East is intended in 1970 to surpass 3 million tons. It is obvious that the Soviets will succeed, because they already receive more than 2.5 million tons from this area. The total U.S. catch from all areas is not much more than 2 million tons.

To summarize, the development of a marine counterpart of the Soviet land giant is proceeding full blast, not only by extensive shipyard orders in Japan and in western Europe but also by a major building program in Soviet shipyards. In the Black Sea and Leningrad areas shipyards are putting out two to three new vessels each month, almost on a conveyor-belt principle. They are very modern ships, and they are adjusted to special needs. Through special air conditioning and potent refrigeration, some are equipped to handle tropical catches. They have also developed new types of vessels for modern-day tuna fishing. These units are much bigger than ours, some of them ten times larger. In terms of the mother ships, the biggest unit the Russians now have is a far cry from the small freezing trawlers of 2400 tons with which they started out. The new vessels, the so-called Vostok units, are 40,000 GRT (gross registered tons), each processing more than 100,000 tons of fish a year. However, the one that seems to suit the needs better and appears to be more economical is actually one half that size. The 40,000-ton ship is actually too large to find waters sufficiently prolific to support that kind of huge monster.

Another great episode on the aquatic front is China's mobilization of its waters. This has been chiefly concentrated on inland fresh waters. I will not review that whole subject, but the coastal fish resources have also been mobilized, expanded, and furthermore supplemented by large-scale cultivation of seaweeds. This undoubtedly is essential for procuring adequate amounts of protein for the survival of the Chinese. Fish is an important supplement to their daily rice diet, and it is really one of their very big undertakings when you look at it in terms of quantity. China today is getting from its fresh-water resources about 3.5 million metric tons a year, and it is harvesting at least 5.5 million metric tons from its coastal resources.

A major oceanic event is the installation of large reduction plants for the production of oil and meal from fish. Such major

bastions have been created on the Pacific coast of South
America—Peru and Chile—as well as on the Atlantic coast of
southwest Africa. The Pacific catching is in the Peruvian Current
off the Peruvian-Chilean coast, and the factories are land based.
Southwest Africa is partly using converted whale-factories as
floating reduction plants.

Some statistical data will indicate the significance of the Peruvian-Chilean takes. More than 95 percent of the catch of Peru
moves into the floating reduction plants, and this is in the form
of a single species, the anchoveta (*Engraulis ringens L.*). The
species is a herbivore and consequently close to the primary production. This catch reached 9 million metric tons in 1964 and 12
million metric tons in 1967. The corresponding 1967 African
catch was 2.5 million metric tons, an annual increase of 225,000
metric tons in the same period from 1965.

In terms of fish quantity, this means that Peru is surpassing
both Japan and the USSR in their worldwide operations. This
says something about the fish abundance of these waters, but it
also is a clear indication of what can be done with purposeful
action. Most of these rich catches are, however, bypassing the
adjacent protein-hungry continents. This applies to tropical
Africa and the resources of the Benguela Current as well as to
South America and the Peruvian (Humboldt) Current.

The oceans are mobilized in this tremendous way to feed the
well fed; no less than 45 percent (1967) of the marine catches are
channeled to fish meal; more than one third serves as food to the
satisfied world; and only 17 percent reaches the hungry nations.
In addition, as regards the Peruvian operation, we are committing
once again the same tragic mistake: we pay no attention to biology. The biologists have made close studies of the productivity of
the water that can be reached by the present catchers. It is important to realize the immensity of this operation, the great numbers of catchers that have been constructed, and the fact that this
has been the chief source of local income and employment. The
labor required in the plants themselves is smaller because they are
highly automated. This big operation backfired in 1964, when the
catches reached 9 million metric tons. The catches started to drop

drastically for each individual ship and fishing effort. The take in the following year (1965) was reduced to 7 million metric tons. Biologists have been saying for at least 12 years that the maximum sustained stock did not allow more than 7 million metric tons.

The fact remains that there is considerable overfishing. But this is small compared to the "potential" overfishing. If you look at the investment that has been made in this industry and consider the number of its ships, and if you add up what catches they could take, the potential of the present investment exceeds a catching-vessel capacity of 20 million metric tons. This partly explains why there is such an economic crisis: fleet owners do not get the return that is required for invested capital. All the way through, this operation exemplifies an irrational, unplanned, and very shortsighted undertaking. It is, furthermore, narrow in scope in terms of the current situation in which a world short of protein exploits the oceans to feed the well fed but allegedly in the name of providing food for the hungry. The news media constantly reiterate that we are working the oceans with the aim of feeding the hungry. The truth of the matter is that the hungry of the world by and large are relegated to the sideline. Ever since World War II, the ocean catches have climbed unceasingly. This is due to the Japanese and Soviet expansion and, in addition, that of China. The major driving force has, however, been the unbroken increase in the reduction plants' capacity to handle larger catches of fish.

A persistently higher percentage of the world's ocean catches has been channeled into the feeding troughs of the rich Western world for the raising of broilers, egg layers, hogs, etc. The essential fact is this: only about 8 million metric tons (720,000 ton protein) of the total yearly catch from the oceans go to feed hungry people.

We are rapidly approaching the point where almost half of the ocean outtake is moving into reduction plants. More than half of the herring catches of Norway and Iceland is flowing into this very channel. This is ominous because it means that the oceans have become the reserve of the well fed. Fish oil has moved the same way; that is, to feed the satisfied world. These oils are part of the raw material used by the margarine manufacturers of western Europe. The U.S. menhaden catches follow the same pattern. We use the meal ourselves chiefly for broilers, but the oil is "sold" to the Netherlands, West Germany, and other countries.

When I read the catch phrase "Freedom from Hunger," I have always asked myself, "Freedom from Hunger—for whom?" It is obviously not for the hungry. Today they get only a pittance of the world's ocean catches. They show some gain, however, in that they are major beneficiaries of fresh-water fish. Subsistence fishing has been developed and expanded in some areas where they also are the main recipients. Otherwise, on the marine scene this high-rate protein is moving away from the needy.

How big is this outflow or net loss to the hungry world? If you take the South American delivery to the world market, a little less than one third goes to the United States and two thirds to western Europe. In terms of total amount of protein, this exceeds by 50 percent (1965 to 1967) the total meat protein production of the South American continent. It is, furthermore, twice the milk production of South America.

We could put the situation into a historical perspective and describe it this way: in the last 300 years, the white man has mobilized the grasslands of the world to his benefit. He has gone all over and taken the prairies and the pampas, the grasslands of Australia, many of the grazing grounds of Africa, including the South African veld—all this chiefly for his own benefit. He has taken very little account of the people who were there originally; he has killed them off, chased them away, or provided them with calories devoid of adequate amounts of protein.

Seen in this perspective, the present large-scale exploitation of the oceans might be called our latest big swindle. As Western white men, this time we are going out to the "grasslands" of the oceans: the plankton pastures. We are mobilizing them, not to feed the hungry, not to feed the continents closest to these lush pastures, but to feed ourselves.

This is particularly ominous when we look at political developments. After World War II, the white man lost his political dominance of the globe. Independence came to about 1.5 billion people, even though we are still holding on to some of their land to provide ourselves with goodies in terms of coffee, sugar, bananas, and cocoa beans. As an excuse, we are still using the nineteenth century concept that this delivery gains foreign exchange for these countries. Analysis, however, makes it abundantly clear that this no longer holds true. The raw material prices have steadily been dropping (ever since 1952, with a slight recovery in 1963) with the deliveries steadily rising. At the same time, the prices of capital goods (machinery and other technical equipment) which the raw materials are supposed to be buying have persistently increased in order to maintain the constantly rising standard of the rich world. As a consequence, the net gain is coming very close to zero. Look at what has happened since 1952: there has been about a 38 percent increase in deliveries of agricultural products, with a corresponding gain in terms of exchange of a pitiful 4 percent.

Note a few other things that have happened. One is the expanding use of freezing. This process has made the fish still more attractive to a demanding market. Freezing is also a first-rate method for preserving fish. But did you ever think about the fact that salted and dried fish have dominated world trade in fish for centuries? As early as the Middle Ages, Europe was depending on salted herring and salted cod. It seems evident that the Portuguese were in the Newfoundland Grand Banks prior to Columbus' discovery of America. The Caribbean area was dependent on salted or dried cod from the New England states—actually the main income of Massachusetts for quite a number of decades.

A recent book about the Spanish Main[1] presents the first description I have seen of the emergence of protein deficiency disease in the Caribbean area. The Spaniards explored there and found people who depended largely on tubers (no less than six different crops). Some got their protein from a little rodent called agouti, but most of them got it from either fish or sea turtles. The

[1] Carl O. Sauer, *The Early Spanish Main* (Berkeley, University of California Press, 1966).

Spaniards—the technical-aid people of those days as well as the rulers and representatives of the purchasing power—bought this fresh meat. They did not need the tubers (having brought with them grains, beans, etc.), but they bought meat to break the monotony of their daily diet. The natives were left with their fill of calories through the tubers, but were deprived of adequate, indispensable protein supplementation. As a consequence, protein deficiency occurred in several Caribbean islands. It has been too little recognized that the population of these islands declined in two steps. It has always been said that the drop was a question of diseases brought in by the conquerors. As Sauer describes what happened, a first step of some decades seems to have been under-mined health from malnutrition caused by deterioration of the daily food. This appears to have paved the way for the diseases which 40 to 50 years later so drastically reduced the population numbers.

Through freezing we are doing something similar today. The white-fleshed fish—chiefly cod and related species—are channeled primarily into the cutting of fillets. The amount available for traditional drying and salting is correspondingly reduced. Processors look upon salting and drying as operations that belong to bygone days, yet these markets are big and unfilled. The switch from salting and drying of fish is readily explained by the greater profit available from the sale of raw fillets. This trend is most evident in Norway, but also in West Germany, even to the point where European markets seem to have difficulty competing with the U.S. prices offered. This aspect need not occasion too much worry. Far more crucial is the fact that for many centuries the needy world has been the chief buyer of such white-fleshed fish! The United States also is the purchaser of a large part of the Canadian catch and production. The needy world, in a population explosion and with tremendous protein needs, thus is deprived of one of the main sources of first-rate, cheap animal protein, a source on which it has long been dependent. This is reason for more serious concern. People do not realize the fact that dried cod is the most perfect fish protein concentrate the world has ever had and probably ever will have.

We talk about all these fish used in the manufacture of meal as if they were "trash" fish—a common U.S. designation. Sometimes these varieties are ambiguously called "industrial" fish. It is further maintained that these fish are really not acceptable as human food—or that most people would not eat them.

Anyone knows this is not true of herring, a first-rate food fish; still it is the main ingredient of the fish-meal production in Iceland and in Norway. The Danes have based their meal manufacturing on sand launce, which in Japan is a highly cherished food fish. Menhaden was well liked in pioneer days and was food for coastal Indians of pre-Columbian America. Anchoveta in its dried form was a staple food of the Incas, yet a U.S. expert at a scientific meeting responded to my inquiry with the assertion: "The Latin Americans will not eat fish, so we cannot do anything about that." My answer was: "It seems strange that with all the modern technology at our disposal we should be so much amiss compared to the experts of the old-time Inca empire." The conquistadors described their big granaries filled with corn, beans dried potato (*chuño*), and dried anchoveta. The Peruvian coast, only rarely harassed by rains, is ideal for the deployment of air drying and dry storage. The Incas also developed a distribution system for their entire Andean empire. Furthermore, I have been through the Andean villages, and I have seen women actually tear each other's hair in a fight over the last fish stick (dried, from adjacent lakes or rivers) left in the local village market. The merchant broke the fish in two; he gave one woman the tail and the other the head. They certainly know the value of fish. They also know exactly how to use it. We have not addressed ourselves to this very important issue.

Here is another pertinent aspect to consider: directly or indirectly, the tuna fishing of the world is very much an American undertaking. This points up the fact that the United States today is the biggest buyer of fish and shellfish. Fishing experts and many fishing periodicals throughout the world question how the United States is going to be provided with fish. We think we have a limited population growth, but consider the fact that tuna sales have been so successful that the annual per capita consumption now exceeds two pounds of tuna flesh. Multiply that figure by our present population of around 200 million, and you will find in excess of 400 million pounds of tuna. This means 800 million more pounds of tuna fish required each year.

We strongly criticize the Soviet Union for expanding fishing operations into many fishing waters on the international high seas, but there is no doubt that Europe and the United States were among the pioneers in such endeavors. The true forerunners were the Basque fishermen, later followed by the British, French, Spanish, Portuguese, and others. They all went to the big Grand Banks and started catching cod there and bringing it back salted to Europe. But on a modern scale, the United States is really the pioneer of this same principle. Around the start of this century the tuna fish industry got started in California, based on catches from regional waters. This undertaking soon reached the point where usual catches were no longer adequate in volume (a state of affairs due in no small part to the success of the slogan "Chicken of the Sea"). The tuna canneries then sent emissaries to Japan to purchase additional quantities to fill the big orders of the U.S. consumer. A lot of strife erupted in California because this import was supposedly "taking the bread from our fisherman."

Actually, U.S. factories could not supply the market and could not fill the demand that had been created. It became necessary to expand tuna fishing. Fleets went farther and farther southward along the Pacific coast. When World War II began, American tuna fishing units were operating all along the Pacific coast of South America down to southern Chile. U.S. vessels are still tuna catching over this entire area, but their catches no longer suffice. After the war, the United States expanded tuna fishing in the Pacific island zone with new canneries built on the Samoas. Yet this was not adequate. U.S. tuna fishing then entered the Atlantic. A big new base was created in Puerto Rico with no less than four major canning factories. Even this was not enough, and a second base was installed in the Boston area to service catches brought in from the northwest Atlantic.

The United States is, however, no longer on its own in catching tuna. It depends on delivery bases in the Caribbean; at least

12 of these are transshipment bases for Japanese-caught tuna which, in turn, is delivered to the Puerto Rican plants. The United States also picks up West African tuna in Dakar to bring to Puerto Rico; these catches originate with Spanish and French units.

In effect, there is no place in the world picture for a second giant of the size of the United States in tuna fishing. Next to the United States, Japan and Italy consume the most tuna, but this country is catching herself more than 40 percent of the specific tuna fish involved in this kind of operation and is consuming 65 percent of the world's canned packs of tuna.

The USSR has launched a tuna drive and built several new units in the South Pacific to serve this new endeavor. A significant innovation is the 5000-ton series, the first of which was delivered by a Japanese shipyard in 1967. This unit carries no less than nine catchers on deck. I think the Soviet is too late, because tuna studies and stock appraisals from the Pacific and Atlantic report evident signs of overtaxing.

If the total catch of food fish in the world oceans were allotted to the United States, it would not provide very much more protein than we are presently eating through meat. This places the oceans in their true dimension and puts the current glib talk about the limitless resources of the oceans into an essential perspective for discussion.

First, let us take the United States scene. I was asked by the state of Alaska to look into its fisheries five years ago and formulate a program for their future development. At that time some 2 billion pounds were being taken annually from the waters off Alaska by Japanese and Soviet fishing fleets. Their catch is composed of redfish, crab, and a considerable number of bottomfish. In addition, Japan harvests salmon at sea. You can read regularly in *Pravda* about the record catches of ocean perch which Soviet vessels are taking from waters off the Aleutian Islands. The Soviet catch is many times the total U.S. take from Alaskan waters and Californian hake. Do not get me wrong; all these activities in international waters are certainly not the result of any infringement of territorial rights. Certain agreements have been made with the Soviet Union about U.S. priorities to the king crab as a "create" of the American continental shelves. Soviet authorities and fishing fleets have so far honored these arrangements to the dismay and surprise of Japan, which is concerned about similar demands for restrictions raised by other countries around the globe.

The most significant contribution which the United States could make in an effort to feed the world would be to turn the flow of food fish away from this nation and toward the world. It should also mobilize effectively its own resources because it has the inner lines—in Alaska and in many other places (for instance, the hake resources of the California coast). The United States not only could reduce its purchasing "grab" on the world fish markets, but it could create a flourishing trade to the needy world. This would be a truly significant aid contribution, so far as nutrition is concerned, and would also aid the gain of U.S. fisheries.

In discussing this idea with Alaskan fishermen, I emphasized constantly the occurrence on the Alaskan horizon of the sizable fleets belonging to Japan and the USSR. I pointed out that it would not be many years before they will be joined by Mexican, Chinese, and Korean fleets. I based this on the assumption that the United States will pursue the policies of not developing its marine fish riches and of not providing the global food market with desperately needed fish and fish products.

The Alaskans hardly believed me, but it did not take two years before the South Korean fleets were there. I can assure you that corresponding Chinese fleets are under construction, and it will not take long before they enter into high-sea fishing and extend their voyages to distant waters, such as those of Alaska.

The fishermen of the contiguous United States and Alaska certainly could and should harvest, produce, and provide the type of fish products that the world needs. Furthermore, we could do it much more cheaply than the big, costly fleets of foreign nations. But this requires the removal of artificial, arbitrary trade restrictions such as those against the USSR.

In this way the United States could fill its own void, too. Exactly the type of white-fleshed fillets which we are currently buying could easily be produced, thereby diverting invaluable fish flesh to the hungry, poor nations. By filling this void from our own waters, we could indirectly help the world. Such action would be in line with our long-range economic interests. It would be a statesmanlike endeavor in the new world which is now taking shape, where food and protein increasingly will be gilded market commodities. There might even be a question of whether protein will not take the place of gold as the key standard, perhaps even become a kind of gauge on the world market. I think we will see the creation of international protein banks.

Ocean fishing, in other words, cannot continue to be the privilege of the rich. High-sea fishing, as it has become developed in the way I have described, is almost as demanding of capital as modern agriculture; thus, it is beyond the reach of the poor world, the two thirds of the globe which has an annual income of less than $200 per person. Yet western and eastern Europe, as well as the USSR and Japan, are forcefully pushing ahead in the construction of hundreds of additional fishing units of all types.

Overfishing, therefore, looms on the horizon, and has already become a serious threat to many species. The only remaining fishing ground of any significance is the Falkland Shelf which, as already mentioned, is rapidly being invaded after a temporary (1968) halt by heavy Argentine fishing fees based on territorial claims extended to 200 miles. Assuredly, the fleets now existing on earth are quite adequate to double the world's catches. It is something to think about. This is the degree to which we are lacking in international planning, as well as in economic consideration, for what we are doing.

Before the shortsighted monopoly of the satisfied world is further consolidated, I think the United Nations should make a solemn declaration that the food riches of the ocean are truly to be considered a common property of mankind. They should not remain a free prey to expanding territorial limits as we see in the ultranationalization of the waters now being pursued. The implementation of such a declaration would and should be to the mutual benefit of all nations. Such an action not only would be the greatest single contribution possible to alleviate world hunger and to fill protein deficits, but might initiate a new era in which world resources would become equally accessible to all people and subject to joint, planned allocation.

Anyone who thinks that the current world protein crisis is going to blow over and take care of itself should remember: the hungry of the world are multiplying twice as fast as the well fed. They will be demanding their legitimate share. They are not going to plead for charity but for simple justice, more equitable division, and sensible sharing of the world's riches.

It is most important that we see the writing on the wall—and interpret its meaning.

The Green Revolution:
Agriculture in the Face of the Population Explosion

James G. Horsfall

The global food crisis is most obvious in the tropics. The temperate zones may have a similar problem before too long because of the population explosion; but their agriculture is so sophisticated that thus far they have avoided the desperate situation of the hungry tropical nations.

The anatomy of the Green Revolution, which began in the United States back in the 1860s, suggests some ways and means by which we can deal with the genuinely crucial problems of food in the underdeveloped nations of the tropics. A century ago, this nation was underdeveloped, too. Ninety-five percent of its inhabitants had to work on the land to feed the rest. Today, we proudly consider ourselves a "developed nation," and less than 5 percent of our population supplies all of us with food. This has been the Green Revolution in the United States. The nations of the tropics must now have some 80 percent of the people on the land. They, too, must shift the ratio if they hope to ease their growling pangs of hunger.

The fantastic alteration in the ratio between the farmer and the rest of the United States' population precipitated an equally tremendous transformation in the ecology of the countryside.

James G. Horsfall has been the director of The Connecticut Agricultural Experiment Station since 1948. A noted expert in the field of plant pathology, he has developed several new fungicides for control of plant diseases and has pioneered in the use of chemotherapy for the control of plant diseases. He has served as president of the Society of Industrial Microbiology and the American Phytopathological Society, and on many governmental agencies in the United States and abroad. He holds three honorary doctorates, as well as membership in the American Academy of Arts and Sciences and the National Academy of Sciences.

People have left the farms and gone to cities. The remaining farmers, of necessity, must get more out of every acre of land; they must treat the land more intensively.

How was our Green Revolution engineered?

A hundred years ago we were emerging from the Civil War. We recognized that the bloody conflict would have lasted only half as long if we had been more highly industrialized. We simply had not been able to produce the sinews of war with our relatively primitive industrial base. We had to have more industries. Clearly, however, it was impossible to industrialize a nation which needed 95 percent of its population in farming. That left only 5 percent of maneuvering room. The labor force had to come from the land; otherwise, industrialization would be out of the question.

The developing nations today face the same problem. They have too many people on the land; they use too many to feed the rest of their populations. We could never have engineered our Industrial Revolution to its present massive state without changing the ratio between agrarian and consumer inhabitants. After all, food comes first. If it should take 95 percent of us to feed all of us, we would not have enough left to operate an industrial society, to shampoo the hair of our ladies in beauty parlors, to teach in Yale University, or to be bureaucrats like me. The farmer-consumer ratio had to come down; this was recognized after the Civil War.

Our grandfathers and great-grandfathers, therefore, decided to uncork a whole new program. They resolved to set up an educational system to deal with the conversion of the United States' population from an agrarian to an industrial base. The system was instituted in 1862. The universities then extant, however, were not geared for adequate participation. Rather, they were equipped to teach the elite of the country: the doctors and lawyers, the statesmen and clergymen, the musicians and artists. A new university system was needed to teach the common man. The nation did not have much capital to put together such a system, so it gave what it had in most abundance—land—to the new academies; it called them land-grant colleges. Those colleges *did* improve the agriculture. They provided much of the capability for industrialization; they helped to pave the way for a tiny minority to feed all of us.

On a population basis, today's ratio indicates that one farm worker in the field can feed 40 people. This really means that only 2.5 percent of all our people comprise the farm labor force. It goes far toward explaining why the politicians take pains to look after our agriculture. With every 40 Americans depending on one farmer, the politicians realize the wisdom of keeping the farmers happy. Some think that they could have done better, but the fact is that farmers do feed us well.

What is the nature of our Green Revolution, of this miracle of five loaves and three small fishes? For an example, consider the State of Washington, one of the big breadbaskets of our nation. From every Washington farmer 40 of us get our wheat, and that wheat is harvested with the products of our advanced technology. Three laborers can run a combine which not only cuts the wheat but threshes it and puts it into bags. Compare that operation with harvesting wheat on a farm in India, where three people and two cattle slowly and monotonously tread out the grain. It is quite obvious why such a high percentage of India's people are necessarily engaged in agriculture to feed the still-famished population, and why it takes only 5 percent of us to serve the same function quite successfully. Look at the difference in land irrigation; compare the Grand Coulee Dam in Washington with a camel walking around and around to pump thin rivulets of water to thirsty crops in India. The efficiency of our farmers is clearly superior; you do not irrigate much land with camels plodding wearily around antique pumps.

In 1798, when the Reverend Thomas Malthus suggested that the world's population would outstrip its food production, the only way to turn out more food was to cultivate more land. What the land-grant college system did was to increase the agricultural productivity in the United States per acre and per man, although the per acre yield did not begin to rise significantly until approximately 1940. It took from 1862 to then for the results of this sustained effort to become really evident.

A striking byproduct of the increased food per acre was the release of land for other uses—new forests, urban sprawl, airports, even Disneyland. Perhaps the most dramatic example is corn. Hybrid corn took over in this country about 1940. That was when we learned how to tailor-make corn to suit ourselves. We could tailor corn for Iowa; we could tailor corn for Maine; we could tailor corn for Florida. Yields per acre shot up fantastically.

We used more fertilizer. Consumption of plant nutrients began to rise sharply in the '40s, and it continues to climb rapidly. This explains why some people complain about the nitrogen in lake waters; they would outlaw use of nitrogen in crop production because some of it leaches out into streams and lakes and raises the algal content. Nevertheless, farmers have found that increased use of such fertilizers is essential to expand and improve their yield of crops per acre. Fertilizers have contributed much to shifting the agrarian/rural ratio so that we could industrialize.

The number of tractors used in the United States began to rise a little earlier than the yield per acre; we learned how to make tractors before we learned how to increase crop harvests. However, the number of acres in production rose until roughly the end of World War II. That is because more land had to be put into use to provide additional food for our allies. With our increased efficiency (much of which originated during the war) we were able to reduce the number of required acres.

What gains did our nation make? We have virtual freedom from hunger; we have two chickens in almost every pot, and this is what Herbert Hoover promised in 1928 when he campaigned for the presidency. Hoover did not have much to do about the two chickens in every pot, but the chicken breeders and feeders did. The curve for chicken production is even steeper than the curves for bushels of corn per acre, fertilizer consumption, or tractor usage.

We are so well provided with food now that some clergymen, saying grace before meals, forget to thank God for the food they are about to eat. The most famous prayer in Christendom says, "Give us this day our daily bread." People still recite the Lord's Prayer, but some include that sentence for the sake of ritual.

They do not think they have to thank God for bread any more because they can buy it at the supermarket.

This nation has the lowest relative food costs in the world. An American family spends a smaller proportion of its income for food than any other family in the world, and the trend is clearly downward. At present the average family in the United States spends less than 18 percent of its disposable income for its food. This has fallen from 22 percent in 15 years. (Canada spends 20 percent, Australia 22 percent, Japan 38 percent, and Ghana 60 percent of its disposable income on food.) This means we have more money to buy television sets and two cars for every family.

Because agriculture needs less land than in the past to feed us, we have built factories on former farmland. We have more land for two-acre dwelling lots, more land for recreation, more land for wildlife preserves and forests. Connecticut has vastly more trees today than it had 100 years ago. Land not presently required for food lies in forests where old stone walls indicate former boundaries of cultivated fields. We have more land for schools and playgrounds, for business, for airports and highways. One day we may need this land back for agriculture, difficult as that would be to achieve, but at the moment we have plenty of land to do with as we wish. These are all characteristics of a developed nation. If agriculture is efficient, the nation lives well.

What has the nation paid for this advance? What is the price of becoming developed? For one thing, efficient agriculture consumes a fabulous amount of fossil fuels. The effect on our food production will be painfully apparent when the fossil fuel supply runs low.

Development of our agricultural efficiency has signaled the death of many small villages; it has caused crowding in the cities as automation of fertilization and harvesting equipment have taken farm workers' jobs. This responsibility is shared by the industries which—like agriculture—have liberated a lot of people onto the welfare rolls. Agricultural efficiency has allowed nitrogen to leak into the water and give us undesirable algae. It has necessitated the increased use of pesticides with all their concomitant hazards which trouble some people. It has lessened the significance of the family; a farm required the cooperation of everybody in a family, from the smallest child who gathered up the eggs to the oldest son whose muscles hastened the task of cultivating. These requirements, which linked family members in a common cause, have virtually vanished.

Will this Green Revolution continue, or will these efficiency curves flatten off? Can we continue to feed an expanding population? By the year 2000 the earth's population is expected roughly to be double what it is now. Can we double our food supply between now and then?

Although the corn yield per acre is still going up, the yield of potatoes—also a staple—is clearly stabilizing. The potato output rose steeply in the 1940s, thanks chiefly to the control of diseases and insects with increased use of organic pesticides. Without those controls, potatoes would be back to their 1940-45 per-acre yield. The flattening curve in our nationwide yield of potatoes is a tiny cloud on the horizon. Other crops will probably soon follow. We will need another quantum jump such as the 1940s' pest control if we hope to boost potato production.

The most dramatic statistical curve I have found recently rather shocked me. We in the United States have always felt that the most important way to increase crop yields is to apply fertilizer. Any home owner with a lawn knows that he will have a pretty scrofulous-looking bunch of plants if he does not put fertilizer on it.

But note this: the nationwide curve relating fertilizer consumption to yield in the United States is clearly flattening! This is a shocking revelation. This does not mean that on a given farm for a given crop in a given year you could not put on more fertilizer to increase the yield. It does indicate, though, that unless we have some other quantum jump in our technology to increase food production, the nationwide increase in the use of fertilizer will produce an ever lessening effect on crop production with the passing years. And, besides, it will release more contaminants into the streams.

Five major possibilities are available to match the food supply to the growing population:

1. We can consume our surpluses of food grains. This country has roughly a year's carry-over supply. If we grew no wheat or corn at all this year, we would still have enough to eat by this time next year—but then it would be gone. We are not going to use all that surplus, however. We are going to continue to carry surpluses. To do otherwise would be foolhardy.

   It has been said that these surpluses are a national embarrassment. A recent book is entitled *An Embarrassment of Plenty*.[1] Of course surpluses create some political problems, but how can we be embarrassed by having plenty? No one, and that includes politicians, would wish to live in a country that could produce no surpluses of food. That is the unhappy position of the underdeveloped countries.

2. If we should use up all our surpluses and begin to have a little difficulty getting enough to eat, we could bypass all of the animals. We could quit growing all of those steers that make such nice steaks, because it takes seven to eight pounds of grain to produce one pound of beef. We could eat the grain ourselves, use up the beef, and quit growing beef cattle. We would gain about seven pounds of food for every pound of beef we slaughtered.

3. We could plow up more land. This is the classical way to handle food supply problems. Roughly 50 million acres are out of production now. (This is a conservative estimate; if you prefer, make it 60 or 70 million acres.) Approximately 300 million acres are engaged in production of agricultural goods. The 50 million-acre reserve means that we have a 16 percent surplus of land, but the surplus land is not as good as the average in production. Farmers do not take out their best acres; they set aside the poorest land. Anyway, even

[1] Lauren Soth, *An Embarrassment of Plenty* (New York, Thomas Y. Crowell, 1965).

though those 50 million acres are not as good as the rest, we could still put them back into production.

However, our highways and our suburbia, our airports and whatnot, are biting off about 1 million acres of land a year, and this goes up annually. (If it were 1 million acres last year, it probably is 1.1 million this year.) Of course, that is not all agricultural land, although agricultural land is probably somewhere around two thirds of the total. We do not build parking lots or many dwellings and highways on the sides of hills; we build them on the beautiful, flat farmland. Even if we assume that only two thirds of the 1 million acres are shifted annually from farms to urban use, we would use up our 50 million acres in less than 50 years, because this rate of transfer is rising.

4. We could do a better job of pest control. Instead of letting weevils gobble up the grain, we could eat it. Unfortunately, this gets us into trouble with our ecologist friends, because it is going to require better and probably more poisonous pesticides than we are currently using. If we fail to control our pest enemies, they will eat the food before we get a chance at it.

5. We could utilize the sun's energy more completely. We could make more efficient use of the green leaves which synthesize the food which we require. Agriculture is a device for capturing the kinetic energy of the sun and converting it into chemical energy; then we eat it and convert it back into kinetic energy. We must develop devices that will improve our plants' efficiency in capturing more energy from the sunlight. In chemical terms, this gets down to studies of photosynthesis: reduce the daylight respiration so that you can use up the carbon dioxide, rather than throw it back into the air. It involves improved physiology of transport of the synthesized carbohydrates out of the leaves and into the grain.

Nobody talks about the tall corn in Iowa any more because about three feet of the stalk was worthless as food for man or cattle. Researchers have found new ways for the sun's energy to improve Iowa's corn and eliminate the waste.

Through a more efficient method of using solar energy, the famous IR-8 rice has been developed in the Philippines.

What about a Green Revolution in the hungry nations?

It has been written that in the tropics the stork has passed the plow. The question is: Can we put wings on the plow so it can fly faster than the stork? Paul Ehrlich, speaking in this series, has suggested clipping the wings of the stork. I do not quarrel with that. This is another device, and we will probably have to use both of them. As a biologist concerned with the food supply, I make it my business to put wings on the plow so that it can fly at least as fast as the stork. To do this we must engineer a Green Revolution in the tropics through education and applied science.

The hungry nations are at the crossroads where the United States stood a century ago. They have their universities as we did at that time, but the teaching of agriculture has a pretty low priority in those universities—as it had here 100 years ago. Commissioners of Agriculture throughout the tropics are not agriculturally educated. That is tantamount to having a farmer for the Surgeon-General. Who would think of putting the Ministry of Medicine in the hands of a lawyer? Yet the Ministers of Agriculture in the hungry nations are most often lawyers or nonagriculturists. Training of agricultural specialists in the universities of the tropics is almost nonexistent. Universities have traditionally served the elite; they will have to educate the common man if they hope to engineer a Green Revolution similar to ours.

Ever since World War II, the United States has been promising to raise the hungry nations out of their predicament by industrialization. We enunciated that policy in the Department of State right after the war. But that puts the cart before the horse. Nobody can industrialize a nation with 85 to 90 percent of the people on the land any more than we could have done so 100 years ago. It has been a terrific waste of our strength; we poured money into industrializing India, and food production declined through the entire period.

Then we adopted a second procedure: the exportation of American knowhow. We would send retired county agents into the hungry nations. We would export our American agricultural technology. Those farmers in Iowa know how to grow good food, we said; now why don't you foreign farmers do it the same way? This operation sadly failed, too. Congress did not learn about it very fast; in fact, it recently passed another edition of the Food for Freedom business and created a section called Farmer to Farmer. It decided to send farmers to carry the knowhow, since the county agents had failed. That program, too, fell by the wayside. This is what I call the knowhow, showhow fallacy.

Why didn't the program work? We can send Jeeps that can negotiate the roads in underdeveloped countries. Why can't we send hybrid corn to help solve their food supply problems? Biologically, the answer is not very complicated to understand. If we put fertilizer—our classical method for increasing yields—on most of the crops of the tropics, we get less yield than if none was applied. This is not always the case, but it is true often enough. For thousands of years the plants growing in the tropics have had no appreciable applications of fertilizer. If a plant had a high-yielding gene, it almost certainly would have been lethal because it would overgrow the rest of its environment. If we come along and put fertilizer on a plant that has lost its high-yielding genes by natural selection, we will damage the plant more than help it. The result: if you tell an Indian farmer to put on fertilizer and he gets less yield than he had before, you lose your lofty position on your self-erected pedestal.

Rudyard Kipling, who spent much of his life in India, understood the futility of such efforts to improve conditions in the tropics. We should have read Kipling back in 1946-47 when we began to say that we would increase the food supply of hungry nations. Kipling wrote,

> The end of the fight is a tombstone white
>   with the name of the late deceased,
> And the epitaph drear: "A Fool lies here
>   tried to hustle the East."

We tried to hustle the East; it did not hustle, but it was really not its own fault. It would have liked to be hustled into a solution of its food crisis. We did not know how to hustle it. We did not know how to hustle it even though we had spent a painful 100 years drawing our own blueprint for it. Actually, I am amazed when I contemplate it. The reason is, of course, that those who drew the blueprint, the nation's agriculturists, did not occupy the high policy seats where the decision was made to industrialize, not agriculturalize, the hungry nations.

I was in India about ten years ago, when our national efforts were at their nadir. There were no agricultural universities in the sense of our land-grant colleges and, therefore, very weak training of agricultural experts in India. The country had its Oxfords and Cambridges (somebody called them "Oxbridge" schools) in which were educated the future lawyers and doctors and clergymen, but few in the practical world of agriculture. Only the Brahmans—the top caste—were educated in India in those days. The Brahmans were supposed to become educated, but not to soil their hands. They could not very well improve the agriculture because that involved working in the soil. And so India remains today a vast nation with a relatively few rich and educated people on top and the multitude of poor farmers with no means of education and a dismal food supply at the bottom. It is now in the process of establishing agricultural universities.

The Rockefeller Foundation has already engineered quite a respectable revolution by using precisely the same technique which we used in this country: education plus adaptive research. It encouraged the establishment of a sophisticated College of Agriculture in Mexico in 1943.

The Foundation's efforts began in that year when George Harrar went to Mexico. He quickly discovered the knowhow, showhow fallacy. He learned that we cannot go down there and transfer American knowhow directly, that we have to develop the technology on the specific site. This principle has since been called adaptive research; it involves "on location" plant breeding, genetics, soils work, and plant protection.

Of course, Harrar's staff started out by trying fertilizers, and they quickly learned that this remedy—so successful in the United States—tended to *reduce* the wheat and corn yields of Mexico. Then they imported some high-yielding varieties of corn and wheat that grow so well in Nebraska, Minnesota, and Iowa. Again, failure; these varieties achieved less yield than the Mexicans got with their own corn, and put on practically no ears at all. They later found out that the diurnal length was wrong. U.S. corn and wheat grow in long days, and the days are relatively short in Mexico's lower latitudes. Besides, the high-yield varieties wound up with all kinds of diseases that they never suffered up in Iowa.

So the Rockefeller Foundation researchers had to work with the measly corn and wheat that they found in Mexico because those varieties were adapted to the day length, the high temperatures, low rainfall, high elevation, and all the rest of the ecological factors involved. They introduced high-yielding genes from Iowa and Minnesota into the local varieties, and then selected the hybrids with both high-yielding genes and local adaptation. It was simple plant breeding, but it had to be done right there in Mexico; it could not be done in Iowa or in Connecticut.

When the genes of the local varieties were sufficiently upgraded, then fertilizer worked wonders as it does in the United States. The Connecticut Agricultural Experiment Station is proud of discovering the principle of hybrid corn, but hybrid corn which will flourish in Mexico had to be developed in Mexico. We cannot successfully transfer the Connecticut strains to Mexico.

Adaptive research is the principle discovered by the Rockefeller Foundation in its work in Mexico. Using this principle, it developed some strains that just about doubled the yield of Mexican wheat. The success in Mexico led the Foundation to decide about 1957 to set up, in cooperation with the Ford Foundation, a similar place—the International Rice Research Institute—in the Philippines.

What did the researchers do when they got to the Philippines? They tried fertilizer. Even after the work in Mexico, they tried fertilizer first. The Foundation had new researchers in the Philippines, fresh out of agricultural America. They put fertilizer on the rice, and grew less rice than they harvested without any fertilizer.

They had to learn the hard way. They acquired rice with high-yielding genes from Taiwan and Japan, and crossed them with the locally adapted plants that did not have high-yielding genes. When they put fertilizer on the resultant strains they tripled the yield.

Somebody once said farmers may be ignorant but they are not stupid. All the researchers had to do was put IR-8 rice, this elegant new variety, in a Filipino's field beside the old indica rice, pile on fertilizer, and wait for results. The farmer wound up with three times as much rice from the new variety. He did not have just 10 percent more rice; you need a computer to tell the difference with such a small increase. A farmer is not interested in computers; he is interested in crops. When he gets 300 percent more yield, he does not need a college degree to see it. He is no fool; he wants that new rice as fast as he can get it. As a result, a vast black market has developed all over the tropics for IR-8 rice.

The same thing has happened with wheat. India's Punjab wheat area is at just about the same latitude as Mexico's. It too is on a higher elevation, and the daylight hours are approximately equal in both regions. Wheat can be transported across the lines of longitude because day length is the same. Thus, Mexican wheat will do as well in India as in Mexico. The yields in the Punjab went up two and three times, and the farmers started a sprawling black market in wheat. When such a black market develops, we know we have hit on something pretty good.

At last we fairly well understand the methodology for improving agriculture in the hungry countries of the world: research must be done locally. On the other hand, shipping American professors abroad for six-month sabbatical leaves is unlikely to produce any appreciable success. The United States has spent a tremendous amount of money doing that with unacceptable results. It does make a nice trip for the participant, but his usefulness is severely limited; he does not do much for the food supply. He may learn a lot about how the "other half" lives, but if his time overseas runs too long he will start worrying about his chances for promotion back home.

The Rockefeller Foundation gives its researchers a year-round permanent business, assuring them that they will not lose their places in the academic line of promotions while they work in the Philippines.

Research people can do dramatic things if they have long-term contracts with built-in provisos that make their efforts abroad a part of the climb up the professional ladder.

The tropics, for all their lush beauty, desperately need a Green Revolution in agriculture. Easing the hunger of those nations will depend on a huge number of factors. A few bright spots have become visible. For the first time, the Philippines are exporting rice instead of importing it at almost unbearable cost—thanks to IR-8. The yields of wheat have doubled in Mexico, in the Punjab, and in Pakistan.

We dare not forget, however, that the population also is rapidly increasing. Food is life, but if we would bequeath to our descendants their full measure of that life, we should remember John Muir's words: "Everybody needs beauty as well as bread, places to play and pray in which nature may heal and cheer and give strength to body and soul alike."

The Search for Environmental Quality: The Role of the Courts

Joseph L. Sax

We have an enormous quantity of rhetoric about environmental quality, and all too little talk about immediate, effective, and direct action programs. If tomorrow we amended the federal Constitution and declared that the earth was a spaceship, it would not stop a single marsh from being filled.

While we sit around at conferences and university seminars talking about the ecological conscience, dredging and filling, excavating and spraying and bulldozing go relentlessly forward. If those of us who are concerned about the degradation of the environment have something to assert, we had better plug into the mundane world of construction and condemnation, of builders and engineers, and begin to say some specific things about specific operative programs.

One very good way to achieve results when someone is doing something of dubious propriety or legality is to ask a judge to order that conduct to cease, under penalty of law. That is action of a kind which has been too rarely considered in our often grandiose plans to deal with environmental quality problems. It is action which centers on the courtroom.

Lawsuits are certainly not going to solve all our problems, but the judicial forum has been seriously underrated and too often ignored as a management institution both by those who are professionally concerned with resource problems and by the courts

Joseph L. Sax is a professor of law on the University of Michigan Law School faculty; he also teaches students at the School of Natural Resources on legal problems pertaining to conservation. His principal area of interest is natural resources law. Under a Ford Foundation grant he is currently investigating the role of the court and legal institutions generally in promoting environmental quality. His aim is to produce a legal strategy for aiding in rational decision-making on the use of natural resources.

themselves. A particular case study may promote some understanding, if only impressionistically, of the range of potentials and limitations of the courtroom in dealing effectively and directly with environmental quality problems.

Anyone who enters a courtroom with a conservation case can first expect resistance from the court itself. The judge's principal thoughts are almost sure to be, "Why did you come to me? Why don't you take your troubles to the legislature? What do I know about all this? This is not a matter for judicial consideration. What reasons can you possibly give for suggesting that I—a judge—should substitute my judgment for the expertise of an agency or enterprise whose business it is to make the kinds of decisions you are challenging? Aren't you asking me to serve as a super-planning agency? And, in any event, what law was broken by the defendants?

"I am not here to enforce the good, the true, and the beautiful; to be the fount of ultimate wisdom and social conscience. I am here to enforce the law. What rule is violated by this highway plan, this dam project, or this proposal to spray elm trees with DDT?"

Finally, the judge will ask, "What damage do you charge has been done to you? Where is the broken arm or the broken contract? I am not a prophet who can speculate upon the ultimate fate of gulls and terns. I redress loss; I do not paint the future rosy."

This may appear a formidable prospect for the conservation lawyer and his client. Be assured that it *is* quite as formidable as it seems. Any forecasts of a revolution in conservation litigation are composed largely of hope and will power.

The fact is that, after six years of litigation, the famous Consolidated Edison—Storm King case involving questions of environmental damage by a proposed power plant along the Hudson River has again been decided for the utility by the presiding examiner.[1] The court which sent the case down for a second

[1] Consolidated Edison Company of New York, Inc., Docket No. P-2338, Presiding Examiner's Initial Decision, Federal Power Commision (Aug. 6, 1968).

trial held only that the previous hearings had been procedurally inadequate and did not really come to grips with the specific issues.[2]

Every highway location case of which I know has been lost, or at the very most has been won on a procedural ground—such as notice or hearing irregularities—rather than on the merits of the case.[3] The pesticide litigations thus far have been largely unsuccessful in the courtroom.[4] A good many cases have been summarily dismissed on the simple ground that there was no right to sue, or that some unavailable and indispensable party was not present.[5]

Why do I think the courts have an important role to play? Why does it seem to me that the general unresponsiveness of the courts to conservation litigation is misguided? How do I think a more appropriate judicial response can be elicited?

The case which I have chosen for an illustration is by no means a typical one. Nonetheless it has several quite special virtues: it was appealed twice to the state Supreme Court, thus providing a variety of judicial reactions to conservation litigation. It involved in this process a complete trial on merits of the conservation resource issue, which is extremely rare. And it was tried by competent lawyers and a judge who was open-minded, candid, and nontechnical in his approach—not rare, but not universal either. The issue in the case was clear-cut enough to disclose how and why the court responded as it did.

[2] Scenic Hudson Preservation Conference v. Federal Power Commission, 354 F.2d 608 (2d Cir. 1965), cert. denied 384 U.S. 941 (1966).

[3] E.g. Road Review League v. Boyd, 270 F. Supp. 650 (D.C., S.D.N.Y., 1967); Nashville I-40 Steering Committee v. Ellington, 387 F. 2d 179 (6th Cir. 1967), cert. denied 390 U.S. 921 (1968); D.C. Federation of Civic Associations v. Airis, 391 F.2d 478 (D.C. Cir. 1968).

[4] E.g. Murphy v. Benson, 270 F.2d 419 (2d Cir. 1959), cert. denied 362 U.S. 929 (1960); Yannacone v. Dennison, 55 Misc. 2d 468, 285 N.Y.S. 2d 476 (1967); Environmental Defense Fund v. Ball, Supreme Court of Michigan No. 51900 (Nov. 22, 1967), and Court of Appeals of Michigan, File No. 4594 (Nov. 13, 1967).

[5] E.g. Comment, Standing to Sue and Conservation Values, 38 U. Colo. L. Rev. 391 (1966); though it must be noted that standing to sue is becoming less and less a problem.

The case is Texas Eastern Transmission Company v. Wildlife Preserves.[6] It involved Texas Eastern's effort to condemn a right of way across Troy Meadows—a tract of land owned by Wildlife Preserves in New Jersey—to install one segment of a natural-gas pipeline. Wildlife Preserves is a private, nonprofit organization devoted to acquiring important natural habitats and maintaining them in that condition for such purposes as wildlife preservation, scientific study, and esthetic enjoyment. Troy Meadows, which was conceded in this case to be one of the finest inland, fresh-water marshes in the northeastern United States, is such a habitat.

Composed principally of marshland with a smaller wooded upland area on its western side, the Wildlife Preserves tract contained two significant developments when Texas Eastern instituted its suit to condemn a right of way. Running essentially north and south in the wooded area was a 50-foot-wide cleared area under which lay another company's gas pipeline, the so-called Algonquin route. In the marsh area to the east was an electric power right of way, where overhead transmission lines were strung on high towers.

Texas Eastern originally sought to condemn another 50-foot right of way in the wooded area, directly west of the Algonquin route. It wanted to clear this area, bring in its heavy equipment to dig a trench, lay its pipe, and then cover the pipe with the previously excavated earth.

Wildlife Preserves objected to this proposed condemnation, but it took neither the position that the pipeline should not be laid at all nor that it should not be laid across Wildlife Preserves land (although it had originally so claimed). If it had asserted such broad defenses, it would probably have lost the case before it even went to trial. Rather, Wildlife Preserves posed a specific and, according to them, ecologically superior alternative. It suggested that the pipe should be laid in the preserve's marsh area along the existing power-line route, and not along the upland,

[6] 48 N.J. 261, 225 A.2d 130 (1966); 49 N.J. 403, 230 A.2d 505 (1967); see McCarter, "The Case That Almost Was," 54 *American Bar Association Journal* 1076 (1968).

forested route requested by Texas Eastern. In support of this declaration—before the case went to trial—and in support of its claim that there should be a trial on the routing question, Wildlife Preserves filed affidavits which briefly sought to explain why the marsh route was more desirable. The affidavits maintained that a route through the marsh would produce less erosion and, thus, less stream pollution than a route through an upland excavation; less disturbance of the vegetative cover and a more rapid recovery of that which would be disturbed; and less adverse impact on limited and needed woodland area. It asserted that the marsh route was feasible as both an engineering and an economic matter, and that it was available.

As the case took legal form, the question was not whether Wildlife Preserves was correct in the claim that its proposed route was superior, but whether it had a legal right to litigate that issue.

Under traditional doctrine the answer has usually been a simple "no." The rule has been that when an agency with authority to condemn land (public utilities, like governments, commonly have that prerogative) exercises its condemnation power for a legitimate purpose—such as a pipeline right of way—the only question open to litigation is the amount of monetary compensation to which the condemnee is entitled. Although this is not an absolutely unqualified rule, the courts are exceedingly reluctant to permit litigation over a condemnation's necessity or wisdom, or over the manner in which the condemnation power is exercised.

Such reluctance is easily understandable. Condemnees are not frequently eager to exchange their property for cash. It would always be possible to argue interminably over the merits of taking tract A, rather than tract B, as a site for a school or fire station, or for putting a highway interchange up or down the roadway, on a neighbor's land rather than on one's own.

Therefore, at the outset, counsel for the condemnee, Wildlife Preserves, was faced with a formidable legal obstacle. He wanted to litigate an issue which—for quite good reason—the courts had usually ruled nonlitigable.

The response of the Wildlife Preserves' counsel was one of

those happy marriages of doctrine and policy which distinguishes the good lawyer from the mediocre. In it lies an essential message for all who want to get the courts to respond to conservation cases.

Courts will generally permit litigation on the merits of a condemnation in one situation: where an agency with the power of eminent domain tries to condemn property held by another agency with the same power. This is not an uncommon situation. Cities, states, highway departments, public utilities, and many other entities possess such power, and they often covet each other's land. In such cases courts may permit a trial on the question of which carries the predominant public interest, the existing or the proposed use. Obviously, without a judicial decision, the two agencies might perpetually condemn and reclaim a particular parcel of land.

Because the power of eminent domain is bestowed only on those bodies supposedly engaged in serving the public interest, it is the issue of greatest public interest which determines judicial conflicts between such agencies.

Counsel for Wildlife Preserves seized upon this doctrine. He declared that the function of his client was also public service, the maintenance of a natural area and its availability to the general public. Therefore, he said, Wildlife Preserves should be treated in the same light as a possessor of the power of eminent domain, and should be permitted to litigate the question of predominant public interest with Texas Eastern.

The idea was particularly felicitous for several reasons. To a court accustomed to thinking, "Our job is to interpret and enforce the law, and not to generate social policies," the defendant Wildlife Preserves said, "Yes, and we are asking you to apply a very conventional sort of law to a slightly unconventional situation which does not change your function. If my client were a public agency—a state park department, for example, engaged as it often is in just such disputes as this—precedent would compel you to do exactly what we are asking you to do here."

To a court which is all too ready to say that it is not equipped to indulge in this second-guessing of technical experts, or to be a super-planner, or believing that it is not competent to choose between birds and people (as many judges think of these problems), this traditional format says unanswerably: "You have engaged in such decision-making for decades, and have done it acceptably; only you never thought of it that way. So, you have nothing to fear in terms of your competence."

Moreover, by claiming that operation of a wildlife preserve is an activity invested with a public interest—as a power company or a railroad is—and entitled to the same consideration at law, counsel indirectly and cleverly moves the court toward that very radical-seeming change which is so often discussed in the abstract and so little made a part of the operative world: putting the concern with preservation of the environment on a footing with the interest in exploitation of the environment.

I have detailed this development in order to contrast it with those arguments which urge the development of an ecological conscience by judges or the recognition of a conservation bill of rights. I am by no means opposed to legislative reform or reformed attitudes—quite the contrary. However, I am dubious that such changes are going to be brought about either by statutory fiat or by a brilliant lawyer's argument. Those who say that we cannot legislate social attitudes—odious as is the context in which such views are often expressed—have a point.

Experience suggests to me that courts will not jump into the environmental quality arena with do-good zeal. They will have to be led gradually, via traditional routes (artificial as they may seem to the layman). They are not only professionally conservative, but they are genuinely and correctly concerned about their competence and their proper role in such disputes.

If judicial attitudes are to change, it will have to be an evolution arising out of accumulated experience—first with easier and more traditional-seeming cases. As the courts recognize both the potentials and the limitations of their competence, and as they educate themselves to feel more comfortable with the substantive problems, I believe they will move on to seek to deal with the problems they perceive to exist.

I do not want to appear to advocate glacial change, because I

personally would like to see some needed jobs get done soon. But
I believe lawyers must work carefully and cautiously in this field,
lest they bring discredit on the cause they want to advance, and
destroy that which they seek to create.

The process thus far described in the Wildlife Preserves case
illustrates the cautious creativity which I believe is needed in this
field. Counsel for Wildlife Preserves extracted from the New
Jersey Supreme Court an extremely significant legal precedent
with good language, with a doctrinal advance, and, most important, with a belief in his client's right to a trial on the merits of
the condemnation issue.

In its opinion the New Jersey Supreme Court reasoned as follows: A public agency subject to condemnation would be entitled
to a trial on whether its existing use is paramount to the con-
demnor's proposed use. Wildlife Preserves does not quite rise to
this status, since it is not a public agency with the right of eminent domain itself. Conversely, even a private person could raise a
claim of arbitrariness, and Wildlife Preserves ought to be viewed
as on a somewhat higher legal plane than that. So, said the court,
inventing a doctrinal middle ground to fit the case:

> [Wildlife Preserve's] voluntary consecration of its lands
> as a wildlife preserve, while not giving it the cloak of a
> public utility, does invest it with a special and unique
> status. Qualitatively, for purposes of the present type of
> proceeding, the status might be described as lower than that
> of a public utility but higher than that of an ordinary own-
> er who puts his land to conventional use. Unquestionably,
> conservation of natural resources would become a legiti-
> mate public purpose if engaged in by the federal or state
> government or an authorized agency thereof. . . .
>
> Under the circumstances and though [Texas Eastern's]
> right to condemn land in this area for the pipeline is clear,
> we believe . . . that Wildlife Preserves is entitled to have a
> plenary trial of its claim that a satisfactory alternate route
> is available to plaintiff which will not result in such irrepa-
> rable damage to the preserve.
>
> We conclude, [that Wildlife Preserves] should have the

opportunity to present its proof as to available alternate routes for plaintiff's pipeline, which defendant claims would better serve the over-all public interest and convenience.

This was a considerable victory. It rested upon two critical factors: the court's ability to satisfy itself that it was performing a more or less conventional function; and the assurance that the case would not be merely a vague debate over vague values, but rather a rigorous comparison between two precise and available alternatives with specific evidence of specific damage to be used to compare them.

It should be noted that it was not necessary for counsel to imbue the court with an ecological conscience. Significantly—and this is a factor which is distinctly underestimated in most discussions of conservation cases—the court was perfectly ready to accept the importance of conservation, as have a number of other courts. That job of public education has already progressed surprisingly far. The problem is to put one's case in a context where a court feels that it is capable of giving recognition to those values within a familiar legal framework. That is the job which was so successfully undertaken in the first phase of the Wildlife Preserves case.

Within a month the case was back in the Superior Court of New Jersey and ready to go to trial.[7] At that point, a whole new set of questions arose: Would Wildlife Preserves really have a chance to establish the relative merit of its proposal, or would it in fact be put to the traditional and virtually impossible burden of establishing conventional arbitrariness? Would the judge be responsive? Would he be able to respond intelligently to the scientific testimony, or would he nervously tap his fingers all the while, feeling that he had a birds versus people case before him? Even with an open-minded judge, could the issues be put into a

[7] The remanded cases are Texas Eastern Transmission Corp. v. Wildlife Preserves, Inc. et al, Superior Court of New Jersey, Law Division—Morris County, Morristown, New Jersey, Docket Nos. L-8612-64, L-13678-64; L-13784-64; L-5853-65; L-5856-65; L-5860-65 (January 1967).

format which would make possible an intelligent decision by a nonexpert?

Even in so relatively simple a case as this there are a multitude of issues which could make a rational decision almost impossible by their incomparability. For instance, if it were found that the defendant was right about the loss of tree cover but wrong about the impact of laying the pipe in the marsh, right about the impact on streams but wrong about siltation, it is not at all clear that a rational decision would be advanced.

A principal virtue of the litigation process is its special sensitivity to the problem of defining issues. It is not simply a forum for the accumulation of information; it is also a mechanism for making decisions. Therefore, it puts a high premium on sorting and sifting a controversy until it settles on the critical facts, so it can appraise the evidence and decide whether the necessary burden of proof has been carried. This is what lawyers call "joining the issue."

As one reads the trial transcript, one can almost see and feel Judge Joseph H. Stamler in the early part of the Wildlife Preserves case struggling to determine for himself not only what the facts are, but what the decisive issues are. He is trying to get the issue joined, to get the case down to a set of facts which are specific and concrete enough for the mind to assimilate and compare, and come to grips with some manageable questions. This is what is unique about the litigation process. If you have ever seen or taken part in congressional or administrative hearings, or in the processes of planning-type commissions, you know how much hot air, unproven assertion, vague denials, and plain obfuscation usually attend the resource decision-making process. In the well-run courtroom, there is no place for such nonsense. If you have an assertion to make, you had better stand ready to prove it; if you have exaggerated, you will pay for it on cross-examination; if your perspective is limited, the court will be apprised of the fact through the adversary process.

The judge in this case was not an expert on the technical questions being debated by the experts. Indeed, at one point in the trial he said, "Before this case started I looked up the meaning of ecology in the dictionary because I noted it in the Supreme Court's opinion. I was not aware of that before." But he *is* an expert in decision-making, and for this reason he was able to make sense out of the controversy. That, after all, is what was required.

For nearly 500 pages of testimony—more than a third of the trial—the judge said little. He listened and he absorbed. He wanted to know the bases of the objections by the Wildlife Preserves people. Finally, he made a tentative decision on that question: they were fundamentally concerned about all the digging up involved in the trench-laying, the erosion and siltation, the loss of vegetative cover.

If the transmission company's activities would truly have an adverse effect on the marsh and the alternate route was feasible and less destructive, Wildlife Preserves probably ought to win. While there had been some testimony about the need for continued wooded habitat for wildlife and about such things as wind-shielding trees, the defendants seemed not to have emphasized those factors and appeared to be unable to adduce any solid evidence in relation to them. Their emphasis was on the excavation problem and its aftereffects.

Now the judge had a manageable problem before him. He was hearing Wildlife Preserves' testimony on the excavation problem, and he would hear Texas Eastern testify on the same issue. He could weigh the two, and he could discover if they conflicted or were compatible. If there was conflict, possibly something could be done to make the damage less serious and reduce the conflict.

The case was not yet over, but at least the judge knew what he wanted to learn. He had plenty of witnesses left on whom to try this preliminary hypothesis about what the case involved. If it did not seem to be working out—if other issues intruded, or if the testimony was excessively inconclusive, he would have to go back and work out another decisional hypothesis.

All that I have just said, of course, is my exercise in mind reading Judge Stamler. But I think that anyone who examines the stenographic transcript of the trial will find it a credible theory.

By the third day of the trial, the judge was ready to test his hypothesis. He jumped in with a question, both to educate himself and to signal the lawyers about molding the balance of the case.

Texas Eastern's lawyer had just finished cross-examining one of the Wildlife Preserves' principal witnesses; the witness was about to leave the stand. The judge interposed:

"I have one question. Stay there for a moment, please. You testified, if I understood you correctly... as recently as 1964, 1965, or 1966 you observed some siltation downstream that you could attribute as coming from the [Algonquin] pipeline right of way?"

A. I saw siltation leaving the pipeline in 1964.

Q. Now, you as one of the trustees of Wildlife Preserves and an expert in the field of recovery and stabilization, what steps did you take between 1953 and 1964-65 to stop that siltation from the Algonquin pipeline right of way?

A. To answer your question, we took none, sir.

Q. Steps could have been taken though, couldn't they? ... Technology would have permitted steps to be taken to preclude the excessive or increased siltation in the lower area of the stream where it became shallow.

A. Yes.

Q. [To the lawyers] Do you have any questions?

Lawyer for Texas Eastern: No, Your Honor.

The Court. I don't know whether my questions generated anything.

Lawyer for Wildlife Preserves. I am pondering, if Your Honor please.

The Court. Take your time.

From this point on the case began to take shape. Wildlife Preserves' next witness was their most impressive, and he brought a new and critical factor into the case. When asked to state his choices on location of the pipeline, he enlarged the original two alternatives to three by saying his first choice would be the use of the old Algonquin right of way, under circumstances where great effort would be made to protect against erosion and to promote revegetation. This was a turning point because it suggested that use of the upland area for excavation was not irrevocably undesirable but seemed to depend upon the conditions of excavation and subsequent maintenance.

Again the judge intervened with a series of questions, among them the following:

"Do you feel that specific conditions can be laid down by a qualified person which would insure an equitable relationship between the ability to construct the line according to your first choice and do the least disturbance to the Algonquin line?"

The judge was now opening the way to consideration of a new alternative, suggesting to the lawyers that they had best pursue this line of thought.

From this point on, it was Texas Eastern's case without doubt. Their lawyer first brought into the case the promise that if an upland route were allowed a number of protective measures would be taken: safeguards against erosion and to promote revegetation, to protect older trees, and to refrain from spraying the excavation area. He narrowed the easement from 50 to 30 feet, agreed that the trench would be open not more than five days, that the soil would be double ditched, aerated to prevent compaction, reseeded and mulched; that no trees exceeding 12 inches would be cut, stream banks would be protected during construction, that there would be no spraying, and that shrubs and other herbaceous growth would be permitted to grow upon the right of way.

Then the transmission company put on its own case, and that clinched its victory. Its prestigious witnesses testified that such protections would be adequate to minimize the harm. Uncontroverted engineering testimony was submitted to the effect that building too close to the existing pipeline was unsafe, so that the desired 30-foot right of way was needed. It was claimed without contradiction that to lay the pipeline in the marsh would require building a large dike for equipment to use as a roadway, which itself would create both siltation problems and the prospect of regrowth of undesired plant life.

Everything was fitting together, and as the case progressed it became inevitable that the judge would decide to grant Texas Eastern its desired right of way with the proviso that the extensive protective promises be kept.

I do not know as a technical matter whether the right decision was made in this case, but on the basis of the record, I feel confident in asserting these things:

1. I know of no nonjudicial conservation controversy in which, after having examined the record, I had so positive a feeling that every party had a fair and forthright chance to present his story to a decision-maker.
2. I know of no other controversy in which the diverse issues were so skillfully shaped and tested to bring the prospect for an orderly and comprehensible decision out of the potential chaos of multiple facts.
3. I am aware of no similar controversy in which the decision-maker—whatever his expertise—had so firm a grip on the relevant facts or was so confidently able to make a knowledgeable decision.
4. I know of no other forum in which assertion has been so skillfully tested by precise examination and cross-examination, with greatly enhanced understanding as a result. There was none of the did-you-stop-beating-your-wife business; cross-examination was used only for honorable purposes.

We all have heard a great deal about the job of resource managers and decision-makers in promoting what Gilbert White calls a "broader basis for choice," a wider range of alternatives. We have heard a lot of such theorizing, but I know of few instances in which resource managing and planning institutions have made alternatives emerge so effectively as in this case.

This Superior Court judge in Morristown, New Jersey, listened and learned. With his decision-making power he stimulated a large utility company into a set of specific and exact promises to conduct its business with substantially more concern for the protection of the conservation resources with which it intended to deal. I would trade his exaction of those conditions for a good many statutes with high-flown rhetoric about public hearings, local participation, concern for resource preservation, and conservation bills of rights.

The Wildlife Preserves case suggests the unique usefulness of the courts as participants in conservation resource controversies. It casts serious doubt on those decisions, particularly in highway location cases, which blithely declare that courts cannot undertake to decide the merits of such disputes. It also suggests that, while not every case is likely to be amenable to judicial resolution, a good many seemingly broad controversies can be made justiciable if they are properly prepared and shaped before the plaintiff rushes into court with complaint flying, and if he learns the lesson of joining issue, presenting alternatives, and preparing scientific witnesses to give testimony a court can understand.

I am sorry to have seen this potentially great case lost. Rarely has an appellate court so nicely set the stage for conservation litigation as did this New Jersey court. Rarely has so open a trial judge sat on such a case. It was a perfect opportunity to prove the litigability of such disputes (and it did, of course, to a substantial degree). But it would have been a much more significant precedent if Wildlife Preserves had prevailed on the merits.

I do not know whether the case was lost because the defendant's lawyer did not do his homework sufficiently well or because his clients did not know their own case as thoroughly as they should have. But coming at the case, as I did, with considerable sympathy for Wildlife Preserves, I left it persuaded that in the trial judge's place, I too would have entered judgment for Texas Eastern.

As one who is eager to promote the sensible use of the courts—not as a panacea for every resource problem, but as an extremely useful and largely disregarded instrumentality for rational management—I am deeply troubled by careless, ill-prepared, and premature litigation which can destroy the credibility of the effort to promote intelligent use of the courts. It is lamentable that Judge Stamler had to end his opinion by saying:

"I must comment that in the testimony here before me I was concerned when Mr. Perkins [President of Wildlife Preserves] stated that the Texas Eastern route would destroy valuable

springs but having accepted the alterative of . . . the Algonquin
right of way, I cannot see why this would not equally jeopardize
the springs except that one of the expert witnesses precisely
measured the springs and found them 700 feet away from the
proposed right of way. I don't want to comment here upon the
refutation by witnesses in open court of almost everything that
Mr. Perkins averred would be the devastating damage to Wildlife
Preserves property. The record is clear."

Unless I have read the record very badly, I find Judge Stamler's statement—though harsh—justifiable. He spent a week trying
this case; the Supreme Court and the Appellate Division of the
court twice considered the case. They made novel law for the
benefit of this trial. Yet, once the way was opened, nothing solid
was ready to stand the test of proof.

Similar cases exist of legal hyperbole by some of our con-
servation-minded brethren. They are defeating themselves by such
tactics.

The critical time has arrived to take a reflective step backway
to caution and responsibility, if there is to be a successful step
forward to a legal strategy for environmental quality control.

The Federal Research Dollar: Priorities and Goals

Emilio Q. Daddario

Those of us who have the responsibility of discussing the subject of federal research support and priorities within science find ourselves seeking to justify its relevance to a society highly involved with science and technology. The year 1968 produced much evidence that traditional justifications for allocating tax dollars to the scientific and engineering community are no longer sufficient. Therefore, a science policy review based on recent events is in order.

1. The National Science Foundation (NSF) budget request was cut 20 percent by the Ninetieth Congress. At the same time the Act was amended to permit support of "applied research relevant to national problems involving the public interest." The Foundation was also charged with being a balance wheel to assure proper support of various fields regardless of mission agency requirements. The challenge to do more with decreasing resources has led to a real crisis in the universities and in the Foundation. Yet there are signs of improvement. For example, the International Biological Program in 1968 underwent a serious legislative review as it struggled to get going. This year its planning and direction begin to take shape, and we see line item support for it in the NSF budget. Laying emphasis on our environment and working with many other countries, this offers exciting prospects for us all.

U.S. Representative Emilio Q. Daddario is a leading congressional figure on science affairs. He is a member of the House Committee on Science and Astronautics, and heads its Subcommittee on Science, Research, and Development. He has been prominently involved in several important congressional studies and hearings concerned with environmental problems. An attorney, he has represented the First District of Connecticut since 1958.

2. The demand for new centers of excellence has generated requests for expensive instrumentation and facilities at a time when all agencies have been hard put to maintain existing programs of institutional support. The 1965 directive by President Lyndon B. Johnson to achieve a more equitable geographic distribution of federal funds has run into the same problem. The have-not regions seem to resent the present pattern to the extent that their legislators take a swipe at federal support in general. This is clear from a study of the debate during the 1968 attempt to limit research grant overhead rates to 25 percent. A nationwide constituency for science would have helped tremendously in fighting off budget cuts, but it does not exist; and paradoxically, the funds which would develop new centers are the first casualty.

3. The concept of a more centralized organization for federal science—some would call for a cabinet-level Department of Science—is being resurrected for debate. Some of the current proposals come from science policy leaders who vigorously fought for multi-agency research funding a few years ago. Why have they changed their minds?

In the new emerging objectives of societal improvement, we are not—at least not obviously—technologically limited. Rather, the principal barriers to progress are political, institutional, and economic—and, of course, the imperfections of human nature. Those charged with the administration of programs in the Department of Housing and Urban Development or the Department of Transportation see immediate service as the first order of business. Technology already in being will be employed. Natural science, rather than being called on for help, is often blamed for the problem. Goals are controversial, and there is even debate over what constitutes progress. Social indicators are inadequate, and therefore a feedback to management of the effectiveness of alternative technologies is very difficult. Problems are significantly different from one locality to another so that a single national solution is often not applicable. The lack of sufficient and accurate knowledge in the research results flowing from the social sciences will be no panacea for society's problems. In fact, President Nixon's Assistant for Urban Affairs, Daniel Moynihan, said recently: "The role of social science lies not in the formulation of social policy, but in the measurement of its results. The great questions of government have to do not with what will work, but what does work."

I was recently asked to speak to a seminar at the Traveler's Research Center on the theme "Acute Social Problems—Can Science Help?" I recalled the sort of challenge that is exemplified by the question: If we can put a man on the moon, why can't we get people home from their work in less than an hour? A little reflection will indicate that one reason is that the National Aeronautics and Space Administration (NASA) actually has a far easier task. I think science *can* help, but the easy extrapolation of the systems approach to social problems is a delusion and should be so recognized at the outset.

Where does this analysis leave us in speculating about the future of federal research and development (R&D) funds and priorities for science? We see that the older programs are turning more toward digestion, application, and diffusion of technology. The dollars for the newer national goals will be committed more to service than to research. The relevance of science is not obvious.

And yet I believe we can make a new case for government patronage which will be stronger than ever before because the health of our nation surely does depend on our ability to exploit our intellectual resources. Let me sketch out a rejustification for science funding and relate it especially to our interests in environmental quality.

The man-environment issue is at the heart of more of our social problems than many of us realize. As evidence that this is so, I was pleased to note the recent report of the National Commission on Urban Problems, headed by former Senator Paul Douglas. A chapter of the report is devoted to the environment, and it states:

> The Commission firmly believes that, no matter what else the nation attempts to do to improve its cities, America will surely fail to build a good urban society unless we begin to have a new respect—*reverence* is not too strong a word—for the natural environment that surrounds us.

The appearance of this strong language in a report which might have been expected to deal strictly with ghettos, crime, housing, and transportation is quite remarkable. It counters the often expressed shortsighted viewpoint that environmental quality, recreation, and natural beauty must take second ranking to the battle against poverty, hunger, and unemployment in solving urban problems. In reality, the total human-environmental system must be improved!

The relationship of nature to civilization is further emphasized by Harvey Perloff in the 1968 Annual Report of Resources for the Future, Inc. He talks about the changing concepts in conservation and economics to include "amenity resources." He states:

It will take quite a wrench in thinking to get away from the commodity view of natural resources and to be able to include in the resources category such elements as air and water of good quality, three dimensional space (including airway space, radio-spectrum space, city land, and underground space) and other valued amenity features of the natural environment. Yet, in our crowded urban age, these are the resources that count.

A third example of the growing social concern for the environment is the report to President Nixon from his task force headed by Russell Train. In urging that improved environmental management be made a principal objective of the new administration, the report noted, "The real stake is man's own survival—in a world worth living in."

Thus, it is clear that environment quality is an issue which competes successfully for public support with national security, space exploration, education, efforts to eradicate poverty and hunger, and so on.

In what ways can science contribute to the national capability for environmental management? To what extent have the unanticipated, unintended, and unwanted consequences of applied science adversely affected the environment? Since multiple demands and uses for air, water, and landscape are at the root of environmental policy debates, how can science help us recognize and reconcile these conflicts? Can we show a high degree of relevance, pertinence, and payoff in taking a portion of the scarce funds available and committing them to basic research?

The answers to these questions hinge on development of a national policy which establishes environmental quality as a top priority goal. The Congress has been taking the lead in bringing this about because it is the only institution with the scope to deal with the broad range of man's interactions with his physical-biological surroundings.

In the Ninetieth Congress, more than 120 members introduced legislation pertaining to environmental quality and productivity. The organization of the House and the Senate into specialized committees resulted in the referral of these bills to 19 different panels. As anyone can see, not only the Executive branch of government requires special efforts at coordination. In order to promote a coherent course of legislative action, we convened a Joint House-Senate Colloquium to Discuss a National Policy for the Environment. On July 17, 1968, under the auspices of the Senate Committee on Interior and Insular Affairs (chaired by Senator Henry Jackson) and the House Committee on Science and Astronautics (chaired by Representative George Miller), congressional leaders met with cabinet secretaries and private-sector environmental experts. The result was a substantial beginning of policy planning.

In a paper summarizing the colloquium we suggested the following elements of national policy:

It is the policy of the United States that:
1. Environmental quality and productivity shall be considered in a worldwide context, extending in time from the present to the long-term future.
2. Purposeful, intelligent management to recognize and accommodate the conflicting uses of the environment shall be a national responsibility.
3. Information required for systematic management shall be provided in a complete and timely manner.
4. Education shall develop a basis of individual citizen understanding and appreciation of environmental rela-

tionships and participation in decision-making on these issues.

5. Science and technology shall provide management with increased options and capabilities for enhanced productivity and constructive use of the environment.

There is an immediate recognition in all this of the need for information and the concomitant operational alternatives to be provided by science and technology, building a broad base of technologic, economic, and ecologic knowledge.

Alteration and use of the environment must be coordinated in a rational manner, and not be left to arbitrary decisions of the marketplace or an insufficiently equipped bureaucracy. Alternatives must be actively generated and widely discussed. Technological development, introduction of new factors affecting the environment and modification of the landscape must be planned to maintain the diversity of plants and animals. Furthermore, such activities should proceed only after an ecological analysis and projection of probable effects. Irreversible or difficult reversible changes should be accepted only after the most thorough study.

Criteria must be established which relate cause and effect in conditions of the environment. Indicators for all aspects of environmental productivity and quality must be developed and continuously measured to provide a feedback to management. In particular, the environmental amenities (recreational, esthetic, psychic) must be evaluated. Social sciences must be supported to provide relevant and dependable interpretation of information for environmental management.

Decisions to make new applications of technology must include consideration of unintended, unanticipated, and unwanted consequences. Technology should be directed to modifying these effects so that the benefits of applied science are retained.

To accomplish this will be a great challenge to research and development. Nevertheless, the direct justification of environment-related research will not be as easy as it sounds. We can make a case for expanding our knowledge of ecology, but more important is injecting an "ecological attitude" into the technical activities of all scientists and engineers—from power plant design to detergent formulation. This attitude should be similar to that which Yale School of Forestry graduates now have as they serve the cause of conservation of our environment in this country in the Forest Service and other organizations.

In a sense, a great deal of work is underway. I say this because research project labels have a way of being adapted to appear to fit current fashions. When we have surveyed the federal agencies for research related to pollution or ecology, some quite impressive dollar totals are built up. This may be due to the old haberdashery trick of turning on a blue light to sell a blue suit.

For example, President Johnson in 1965 asked the Office of Science and Technology (OST) and the Bureau of the Budget to recommend "how the Federal Government may best direct its efforts toward advancing scientific understanding of natural plant and animal communities and their interactions with man and his activities." A survey of existing R&D projects was undertaken. The subsequent OST report states, "It is likely that agencies, in responding to the inquiries, interpreted the 'ecological' aspects of their missions rather generously." At any rate, 10 agencies reported a total of $175 million in such work during fiscal 1966.

An independent study presented to our House Subcommittee on Science, Research, and Development in 1968 by the federal Council for Science and Technology Committee on Environmental Quality showed that federal expenditures for pollution-related research, development, and demonstration including pesticides totaled $250 million. I would expect these dollar amounts to increase somewhat in 1969, both from actual additional projects and from the identification of other R&D as falling under the ecology category.

Many scientific and engineering disciplines are also contributing. The range of research includes industrial process variations, food and fiber production, pest control, taxonomy, soil and water conservation, effects of pollution on man, animals, plants, and materials, monitoring and surveying environmental status, and abatement techniques. The agencies involved include the AEC, NASA, TVA, NSF, the Veterans Administration, and the Departments of Agriculture; Commerce; Defense; Health, Education, and Welfare; Housing and Urban Development; and Interior.

This retrospective analytical look at the R&D budget reveals the diversity with which science can serve a broad public need. Unfortunately, this relevance is not readily apparent to budget cutters who want to take an across-the-board whack at the so-called $17 billion R&D fund. It is admittedly difficult to break out and regroup research around all the different social problems without double counting. However, I believe more studies of this sort would clarify the relevance question. These analyses would show that considerable support exists and would point up research opportunities which could attract more funding.

At the same time, thinking about science in terms of national goals should stimulate some researchers to tailor their personal curiosities somewhat. I do not think it is an affront to scientists in this day and age to make such a suggestion. In considering the 1968 amendments to the National Science Foundation Act, we received testimony that the distinction between basic and applied research has become increasingly vague and not particularly useful. Often the categorization depends on the frame of mind of the investigator. In some cases, the course of scientific development is so rapid that the basic and applied stages run together and cannot be separated with any real meaning.

We felt that the continuity of effort and the capability to expand new knowledge should be clearly within the authority of the NSF. The bill provides latitude (which did not exist in the previous law) for the director to exploit areas of opportunity arising from basic discoveries and to support appropriate applied research. It is not our intent that the Foundation support applied research at the expense of basic science. The amendment is permissive, not mandatory. But we do believe that scientists everywhere are alert to the great needs of society and that attention to these needs is not incompatible with continuing federal patronage of *good* research—whether you call it pure, free, undirected, basic, fundamental, exploratory, or applied.

Let me outline a rationale for government support which depends less on direct relevance. I believe this additional justification is necessary in academic institutions in order to gain the sustained resources for science which are vital in terms of research results and manpower training.

When scientists insist that their work is pure and devoid of application motives, they are naive to expect substantial portions of our tax revenues to be devoted to their projects. These same scientists sometimes represent science as a peculiarly noble human endeavor, ranking with the fine arts in challenging the intellect and talents of man. Within the framework of our political system it is difficult to justify expenditure of large amounts of public funds for the purely personal satisfaction of curiosity— merely for the sake of knowing.

Therefore, I am indebted to an article by Lawrence Becker in *Zygon, Journal of Religion and Science* (September 1968), for calling my attention to the usefulness of even the most aimless pure research. His article is entitled "Is Science Moral?" In it he states that regardless of the intention of the scientist himself, it is impossible to think of *irrelevant* research, so pervasive is science in the activities of society. Applications of the most abstruse physical theory and the most esoteric mathematics are persuasive evidence that this is so. Further, he says, "pure science is one of the ways we have of transcending ourselves—of transcending the boundaries defined by our present knowledge and problems and circumstances." Unless we occasionally obtain a really new approach or a novel theory, technology is limited to the tools and materials at hand. Becker concludes that science is indeed "an endeavor of the very highest human morality [because it] is one of the best ways we have of escaping the trap of our current expectations, dilemmas, and resources."

A less philosophical justification for basic research is also becoming available. The National Science Foundation has released a report entitled "Technology in Retrospect and Critical Events in Science," which happily forms the acronym TRACES. This report identifies the key events that led to a number of major technological innovations. It concludes that approximately 70 percent of the necessary precursor knowledge for these innovations originated in undirected basic research programs, often 20 or 30 years before application occurred. One of the innovations studied is matrix isolation, which I understand to be a valuable new technique for studying chemical reactions. The report states that matrix isolation will aid in the solution of the air pollution problems stemming from fuel combustion. The historical trace shows basic research events critical to this technique dating back to 1849!

The other technologies traced are magnetic ferrites, the video tape recorder, the oral contraceptive pill, and the electron microscope. In each case, the report concludes, "The diversity of research which goes to support an innovation, the variations in timing of non-mission research with respect to innovation, and our inability to forecast the nature of probable innovations preclude the possibility of relating most non-mission research to innovations in advance." However, I would add that we certainly have more than just blind faith upon which to base our expectation of payoff from research. History has shown time and again the enormous return on these investments. But the immediate and urgent problems tend to depreciate these long-term benefits unless we are constantly reminded of them.

A few words are in order for those who charge scientists with dereliction of duty for not applying their exceptional talents in a direct way to society's most crying needs. I should like to point out that more realization of a problem's existence and a desire to work on its solution does not in itself insure that effective progress will be made, even if sufficient funds are allocated. Physicists in the past spent much unproductive effort attempting to perfect a perpetual motion machine. We read daily in our newspapers about the failure of well-intentioned social programs, which through their inefficiency and ineffectiveness have deprived the poor of resources the nation thought it was providing to break their cycle of poverty. The common thread we find connecting these widely diverse failures is *lack of knowledge*—knowledge which historically emanates from sources and disciplines that cannot be accurately predicted. Undirected research, in the physical as well as the social sciences, may well be our most helpful course in finding long-term solutions to the problems of society.

In summary then, I see the need for considerable and sustained effort on the part of scientists and engineers to show the relevance of their work. In this regard, communication to the political arena has improved greatly in the past few years. The channels to the Congress are open and receptivity is good. The case for federal support is there to be made. If those concerned with science can be as diligent and innovative in demonstrating their contributions to national priority objectives as they have been in pursuing their technical activities, the strength of American science and technology will continue to grow.

Man Against Nature:
An Outmoded Concept

Clarence J. Glacken

Outmoded means out of fashion or obsolete, no longer able to fulfill a proper function. I am not certain, therefore, that the title of this discussion is a precise one. For outmoded does not mean tired or lacking in energy or virility. The world is full of outmoded ideas which are still very strong and give no indication of dying off.

The topic of this lecture, including its subtitle, opens up themes so vast that their full analysis would carry us deeply into the history of thought, not only Western thought but all thought. The title, however, is much more than rhetorical, for some concept of the man-nature theme and the man-nature relationship is part of any philosophy of life or any world view.

"Man against nature." "Man's mastery over nature." These dichotomies are often thought to be the only important concepts in Western civilization expressing the relationship between the two. Frequently, the "Western" concept of dominance or opposition has been contrasted with "Eastern" concepts of harmony and union with nature, but I believe this contrast oversimplifies matters. Like all other great civilizations, Western civilization is not monolithic in its summations, and it has nourished all sorts of different ideas. There is no question, however, that the man-

Clarence J. Glacken is professor and chairman of the Department of Geography at the University of California (Berkeley). His chief interests center on cultural geography, the history of ideas of nature and culture, and the Far East. He has participated in three international symposia concerned with man's effects on the natural environment, and has served as field associate in anthropology in ethnological investigations of the Ryukyu Islands sponsored by the Pacific Science Board of the National Research Council. He has been a Fulbright research scholar to Norway and a Guggenheim fellow, and has written many articles and two books in his area of studies.

nature dichotomy has been and continues to be extremely important and, although challenged, it has held its own in popular
thought and has, in addition, diffused to many parts of the non-
Western world.

I have the impression, however, that the concept of man
against nature is not typical of the history of thought as a whole,
or of the ideas of prehistoric and so-called primitive peoples. And
even if one has reservations about applying the I-Thou, I-It concepts of Martin Buber, as some have done, to the relation of
prehistoric and primitive man to nature, I think it comes closer to
the mark to say that these peoples thought of themselves more as
identified with rather than pitted against nature. This was one of
the conclusions of Henri Frankfort and his colleagues in their
work, *Beyond Philosophy* [1] : in contrast to modern man, prehistoric peoples enjoyed a close, lively association and identifica-
tion with nature—as if it were a "thou" instead of an "it." This is
an interesting approach, but we still know too little about the
matter to make distinctions. The area is still poorly explored, but
the evidence seems to indicate a widespread feeling of closeness
of human to other kinds of life; see, for example, Colin Turnbull's description in *The Forest People* [2] of the attitudes of the
pygmies of the Congo toward the forest in which they lived. This
probability is reinforced by recent ethnographic studies which
emphasize the intimate knowledge that primitive peoples have of
their environment.

The idea of man against nature is thus, in my opinion, more
parochial than universal. Admittedly it has achieved great
strength in Western thought, but we must recognize that it is
parochial because, despite powerful influences toward uniformity
of ideas through mass media, other non-Western cultures, with
their own values, still exist. The recognition of such parochialism

[1] H. and H. A. Frankfort et al., *Beyond Philosophy, the Intellectual
Adventure of Ancient Man: An Essay on Speculative Thought in the Ancient Near East* (Harmondsworth, Middlesex, Penguin Books, 1954).

[2] Colin M. Turnbull, *The Forest People* (New York, Simon and
Schuster, 1961).

forces us to ask why and under what circumstances the idea of man against nature grew up and has prospered until this day.

One reason for the lasting strength of the idea has been that in modern times it became, in variant forms, the basis for a secular philosophy of history. In this philosophy the course of civilization was seen as a movement, an evolution from a time in which man was under the control of nature to a point at which the situation is reversed and man is in control of nature. The interpretation is closely tied up with the desire to ameliorate the human condition by cultivating the arts and sciences, an idea which gradually developed in the eighteenth and nineteenth centuries into the idea of progress, progress often but not always being seen in terms of both a divorcement from nature and a mastery over it. A primordial harmony was assumed before the coming of man, but man in his progress would gradually humanize the world, creating through technological inventions an even more exalted harmony through his struggles and labors.

I would distinguish between two traditions of the idea of man against nature in Western thought, the first being derived from the Old Testament, especially Genesis 1; the second, a product of modern times, for which I would cite the philosophy of Francis Bacon as a convenient marker without insisting that it is the actual place and time of origin.

The lines of Genesis are indeed striking. In Genesis 1: 20-28 a distinction is made between the acts of God with relationship to all life except man and the acts of God with relationship to man. In the one case, all life is to increase and to multiply; in the other, man is not only to do the same, but also to "have dominion over the fish of the sea and over the birds of the air and over every living thing that moves upon the earth." This is reaffirmed by God after the flood and a new start for the human race with Noah, his three sons, and their wives.

These Genesis verses have taken on a new and ironical meaning in recent decades and in the immediate present because much has been learned in the last century about culture and environment, especially the effects of the former on the latter. The acts of man ranging from deforestation to air pollution and nuclear warfare and the multiplication of man have given dramatic proof of his obedience to the orders of God for all life to multiply and for human life, in addition to multiplying, to have dominion over the rest of the creation.

Observers, especially non-Western ones, have cited the Genesis passages as criticism of Western civilization and its great preoccupation with man and his struggle against nature. I think this analysis is in error because the matter is much more complex. Certainly this theme as it comes from Genesis and from other Old Testament texts continues to be important to the present. Pope Paul VI's Encyclical letter "On the Development of Peoples" (1967) reasserts the truth of the Genesis statements concerning the earth's creation by God for man in its statement that the earth's resources should be developed responsibly, intelligently, and justly. In a striking persistence of ideas, the condition of mankind today is thus linked closely to the Genesis doctrine.

In my opinion, however, the historic juxtaposition of man against nature depends much more on modern thought and on more secular ideas. Without ascribing origins to them (perhaps for these we should look to the history of alchemy) I would cite three thinkers of the sixteenth and seventeenth centuries who expressed this concept at a time when it was more creative than it is at present: Bacon, René Descartes, and Gottfried Wilhelm von Leibnitz.

One of the most famous apothegms of Bacon was that we cannot command nature except by obeying her, and perhaps here we should think of "obeying" as implying "knowing" also. There are many pertinent illustrations but I will confine myself to *The New Atlantis,* in which one sees a philosopher ambitious to reject the scholastic philosophy as a teaching of inactivity, to promote the arts and the sciences, encouraging invention in order to change nature and to adapt it for human uses. In *The New Atlantis,* Bacon compares the great voyages of discovery which have opened the horizons of man with the continued narrowness of man's intellectual vision. Thus, it is essentially a program for the control of nature by man, a creative broadening act comparable in spirit to what he saw in the voyages of discovery.

In that vividly autobiographical philosophical text, *The Discourse of Method,* Descartes tells how he meditated on the inadequacies of the scholastic philosophy. Like Bacon and Leibnitz, he saw knowledge as the key to human betterment. Notions of general physics are intertwined with the good of man. We must have practical knowledge in order to gain ascendancy over speculative philosophy; we must know the elements—fire, air, earth, and water—as well as we know the trades of our artisans and "thus make ourselves, as it were, the lords and masters of nature."

In Leibnitz the philosophy is even more explicit. This indefatigable, rich, and noble mind saw the earth as a divinely designed planet; he was untiring in his hopes for ameliorating the lot of mankind, and mastery over nature was beneficent, a mark of progress. His is one of the most exalted attempts to correlate the progress of civilization with earth's gradual development by human hands as a habitable planet. The advancement of mankind was intertwined with the cultivation of the earth, and it became a mirror of man's enterprising attitudes. In his work, the idea of progress is linked with the idea of control over nature: as man progresses, the earth under his guiding hand will become even more perfect.

If this admittedly incomplete analysis is correct, the early modern form of the contrast between man and nature was viewed less in terms of struggle, more in terms of creativity, and for two reasons:

1. The struggle with and the control over nature were ways of depicting the progress of civilization. In its material aspects, civilization meant this—the purposive changes in nature, the overcoming of natural obstacles by bridges, drainage, roads, and later by railroads and air and sea routes.

2. There was little awareness or study of the age-old cumulative but unnoticed effects of man's activities in changing the environment. There is ample evidence of local awareness but such knowledge was not widely diffused. Lacking is that crescendo of complaint, based on ecological theory, about destruction of the environment by man so characteristic of the last 100 years and

now so common that it appears in articles in *Science* magazine, in Sunday supplements, and in presidential addresses.

By the nineteenth century some glaring inadequacies of this idea were apparent; they are still. We can regard one phase of the romantic movement, despite its complexity, as a rebellion against the dichotomy between man and nature. In the movement for the protection of nature, we owe much to romantic ideas of the beauties of untouched and remote wildernesses, and of the importance of being conscious of our attitudes to the natural world.

In the nineteenth century, the idea of man's control over nature or man against nature was closely linked with the idea of indefinite and inevitable progress. Even today its vitality, I think, is owing to its association with vague, popular, poorly examined notions of progress, even if this progress has no more meaning than that a statistic of the current year in some desirable category is greater than it was for the previous year. Technology and invention were grist to this mill because they represented clear and easily verified successes. Lines in Alfred Lord Tennyson's "Locksley Hall" (as John Bagnell Bury has pointed out in his *The Idea of Progress*[3]) expressed his faith in progress—in the control over nature—as colorfully as any. When Tennyson wrote about his trip in 1830 on the first train from Liverpool to Manchester, he said he thought the whole world ran in grooves: "Then I made this line: '[Forward, forward, let us range,] Let the great world spin for ever down the ringing grooves of change.' " The optimism was based on material progress, on the idea that this high rational civilization in its onward motion not only advanced itself but was producing humanized environments which went along with it. It is true that especially toward the end of the century a literature questioning technology and its effects began to take form but, on the whole one sees in Western civilization of the nineteenth century the apogee of faith in science and technology—under the rubric of "control over nature."

In the second half of the century, however, the seeds of alter-

[3] John Bagnell Bury, *The Idea of Progress: An Inquiry into Its Origin and Growth* (London, Macmillan and Co., 1920).

nate views were planted—and while these origins too are complex and, if pursued, would lead us far afield, I wish to discuss three works that are symptomatic of things to come: Charles Darwin's *The Origin of Species* (1859), George Perkins Marsh's *Man and Nature* (1864), and Charles Dickens' *Hard Times* (1854).

Before doing this, let us look a little farther into the inadequacies of the above detailed idea which were already apparent in the second half of the last century. If we grant that a world view in any culture must rest on some conception of the man-nature relationship, whether it is a religious, economic, or esthetic one, or a combination of these and others, then we can say that in the middle of the nineteenth century the concept revealed shortcomings as a unifier of a body of ideas and its concomitant knowledge.

These shortcomings have in the main survived to the present. What are they? First, the concept is narrow and restrictive—and subject to the same criticism of the conception of man in the earlier traditional concepts of design and teleology. To say of the earth that it has been designed by a Creator for the sake of all life is one thing; to say that it is made for man alone and to use as he sees fit is another. The anthropocentrism of the latter is narrow and crippling. In the secular versions, which follow, the narrow and crippling anthropocentrism continues in the assumption of universal utility for man. All nature becomes a resource.

Furthermore, the emphasis was on the dichotomy, on two worlds, the world of man and the world of nature. I believe also that the dichotomy encouraged the study of man within the framework of human institutions alone, his struggle with and his control over nature, being activities carried on within the purview of these human institutions. It tended to discourage an organic view; beauty, variety, plentitude could be celebrated in art, music, literature. It encouraged a utilitarian view of nature, not a preserving or conserving one; the former was progressive, the latter romantic, an incurable clinging to the past. But its most misleading aspect, especially when it was an indistinguishable element of the idea of progress, was the high plane on which it placed man and his institutions. He dominated nature by rationality and purpose.

Too much rationality was assumed in the changes that brought about this control over nature, this progress. Mastery was the mastery of intelligence and planning. One feels in reading the optimistic literature of the period that the rationality of civilization was taken for granted. The belief was widespread that a great gulf separated primitive peoples and the peoples of European cultures. We now know—it was known then too by many—that the assumption of rationality in civilization is very misleading. Today there is too much evidence to the contrary—so overwhelming that it requires little discussion. The assumption of rationality, that Western civilization was at the apex of civilizations in the march of progress, implied that mastery was rational mastery, that masters of nature were rational masters.

Let us now return to the three works I cited above. I admit my choices are capricious, but the trends they express are not, for they undermine correlations about the growth of civilization and the humanizing of the environment, the usefulness of the man-nature dichotomy, and they place esthetics and natural beauty in an entirely different context.

In the dreary argument over phylogeny, in the sharp debates over evolution and special creation, in the dramatic discussions of the struggle for existence, in the equally dreary and unimaginative attempts to transfer the struggle for existence to human society, what now stands out more boldly in *The Origin of Species* than when it was written is that the theory reasserted in modern evolutionary, not religious, terms the case for examining the interrelationships in nature. These were seen on the model of a web of life. The fact that such interrelations exist in the organic world did not have to await Darwin's exposition; they were part of the design argument, and at the basis of eighteenth-century observations in natural history. God in his wisdom had made the earth and all the living matter in it as a part of an overall rational design, and it was to be expected that everything would fit, that there would be intricate interrelationships in the natural world, replete with adaptations.

But Darwin saw balances and harmonies in nature, webs of life—today we call them ecosystems—as the result of evolutionary processes, products of time, circumstance, selection. This restatement of the concept of a unity and harmony of nature provided the basis for the building of modern ecological theory. In the cats-to-clover chain, the number of cats is related indirectly to the number of mice, bees, and clover, but it is also related to old maids, and the growth of Scotch fir is related to man's grazing animals and the building of fences. A fresh opportunity was created for reconsidering the question of man's place in nature—not vertically as was so popular at the time in the sense of his place in a hierarchy of being (T. H. Huxley's *Man's Place in Nature* is a good example) but horizontally, his activities as part of the organic world as well as of an economic, social, or political world.

The second work, Marsh's *Man and Nature*, was published five years after *The Origin of Species*. Marsh was one of the great American students of the natural environment. He was the first American Minister to Italy, appointed by President Lincoln, continuing in his diplomatic post from 1861 until his death in 1882. The Mediterranean and its adjacent lands were his great teachers—of the power of man to modify the natural world.

Marsh also used the idea of a balance or harmony of nature, not in the way that Darwin applied it (as a general concept bearing on a theory of evolution) but as a measuring device for gauging the force of human agency in modifying the environment. He was concerned with historical questions: the effects of domestication, deforestation, and the control of water and sand dunes. Many of the effects of human interference with the environment were unsuspected, and the vistas thus opened were far broader and deeper than the narrower confines of the idea of purposive control over nature.

Implicit in Marsh's work is the idea that earth history since the coming of man could be written in part as the history of cumulative change by human agency. In this view he had been anticipated by Count Buffon in the eighteenth century (in the seventh of his magnificent *Epochs of Nature*). Human history, observed Marsh, may be the history of man's gradual divorcement from nature; but it is also the history of displacements in the organic world, of the habitats of plants, animals and primitive peoples. Domestic plants and especially animals became extensions of human agency, of human will. The result was to suggest the poverty of history written within the human framework alone, the poverty of interpreting such changes as chapters in economic history. The great theme was that the cumulative force of human agency could be irreversible, could bring about such deterioration that the planet could become uninhabitable.

But why Dickens' *Hard Times*? Because of Chapter 5, which contains the famous description of Coketown—an ugly brick town, its canals black, its river purple with dye, its monotony of activity and appearance. Large streets were like one another; small streets were even more like one another. So were the jobs. Everything was "severely workful." Things were painted alike, people thought alike, everything was accepted as fact—the M'choakumchild school, the hospital, the cemetery. We see here a new type of life based on an industrial creation of brick, uniformity, conformity. Everything in the description of Coketown points to the imposition of values on an urban industrialized landscape, the creation of a new and unique way of living. Coketown is symbolic and symptomatic.

We can discern a similar viewpoint in the words of many other sensitive observers. To the French geographer Élisée Reclus, for example, the positivist tendencies of the day, the desire for progress and technological advance, were creating unique and ugly landscapes. The march of progress, the preservation of beauty were not the same. Is it any wonder, as Lewis Mumford has pointed out in his *City in History,* that such new landscapes produced their own reactions? How else can we read parts of Ruskin, the attempts by men like Augustus Pugin to idealize the medieval city? The cries for the preservation of beauty, for the old in the city, town, or village, were as strong as they are in many parts of the Western world today.

The Dickens description gives us a feeling for newly created and unique industrial landscapes and brings into entirely new perspective the esthetics of landscape. The web of life suggested by Darwin provided new opportunities for interpretations of the significance of the idea of balances and harmonies; it was the latest attempt to find a construct for the study of the natural world. Marsh made vivid and clear the strong interconnections between the nature of man and human culture and the environment; he showed that civilization inevitably has not created and will not create new and rational harmonies in the natural environment.

The web of life, Marsh's historical geography, Dickens' Coketown are hard to fit into concepts of man against nature or of man's control over nature. It is true that their insights could be ignored. The web of life could be relegated to science. Deforestation, erosion, drainage, river diversion could be referred to engineers. Canal blackness, the purple river, the chimneys, M'choakumchild school, and conformity could be dubbed nuisances that time and progress would correct.

In the latter part of the nineteenth century, the web of life, the realization of the historical depth of human agency in changing the environment, and the creation of unique industrial landscapes showed the need for a deeper, broader, more meaningful interpretation of man's place in nature—not, I repeat, his place in the hierarchy of life, but his place in a physical environment with its interrelating linkages much altered throughout the world, and altered for different reasons and in different cultural traditions.

I do not think these ideas were assimilated in the nineteenth century; in retrospect, however, the three examples exhibit tendencies toward undermining the comfortable idea of progress in terms of man's progressive control over nature. These tendencies also weaken the idea of progress as part of a broad teleological development in which civilization advances, the environment with its resources supporting it.

Thus, a gradually developing body of thought which recognizes that civilization might be progressing or at least changing while the environment might be deteriorating obviously confronts man with a new set of circumstances. Modern pessimism, alarm, and dissatisfaction with the concept of man against nature accompany a loss of faith in progress that has become widespsread in this century. Too often civilization means a destruction and chaos of nature, not a softening and a rationalization of it. Today we do not need ideas or philosophies to tell us this. None of us would automatically embrace a declaration that environments become more beautiful as civilizations advance. Our eyes, our ears, and our noses tell us quite the contrary.

Two recent studies show the continuing pertinacity, strength, and allure of the idea of man against nature in contemporary thought. In an unpublished paper, "The Origins and Development of the Marxist Concept of Man-Nature Relationship," which Ladis Kristof prepared for the Far Western Slavic Conference at the University of California at Berkeley in 1966, he shows the decisive role of the idea of man's mastery over nature in Marxist thought from Marx himself to the present. The origin he traces to certain interpretations of the philosophy of Francis Bacon. He cites the relevance of G. W. F. Hegel's work on esthetics, especially his distaste for the view that works of nature are superior to those of man, for it is consistent with the view that man strives creatively through the mastery of nature to create a better society. Kristof continues the analysis from Bacon and Hegel to Nikolai Lenin, Joseph Stalin, and more recent contemporary rulers of the Soviet Union to show the importance of this philosophy in Soviet thought.

Equally striking is an article by Rhoads Murphey, "Man and Nature in China," published in the journal *Modern Asian Studies* I, (1967) 4. It is particularly interesting because it is pertinent to the history of this powerful group of ideas centering on the dichotomy of man and nature. In the following excerpt, Professor Murphey describes the extent to which the 1949 revolution has changed traditional Chinese attitudes toward nature:

In at least one fundamental respect, however, the conquest of 1949 has, in the Communists' own phrase, turned on its head a set of assumptions and attitudes which were of basic importance in the traditional system and has replaced them with a reverse set which may be of equal importance in contemporary terms. This is the revolution in the conception of man's relation to his physical environment. The dialectical conflict and struggle of the 'permanent revolution' which is the touchstone to so much of contemporary China has replaced traditional notions of harmony and adjustment which underlay equally much of the traditional order. In no respect is this radical change more apparent than in the attitudes toward nature.

The Chinese example is particularly striking because of the age, cultural richness, and continuity of Chinese civilization. Chinese history, philosophy, and art afford many illustrations of ideas of a balance and harmony of man with nature, respect for nature, the role of nature in the life of man. The Chinese developed a nature philosophy, *feng-shui*—wind and water—in which there was a very close correspondence between the features of the landscape and cosmic influences, an amazingly intricate system of interrelationships which was the basis for the proper selection of house and grave sites. Recent reports from Hong Kong indicate that it is still important in regions of Chinese cultural influence. The strong place of nature studies and the love of nature in landscape painting, the long respect for tillage and the orderly conversion of the environment—all of these are a part of traditional Chinese attitudes toward nature, attitudes which Murphey's study shows are being consciously and purposefully changed in favor of the idea of struggle and mastery derived from Marxist thought.

It will be most interesting to see to what extent this restatement of the case for a philosophy of struggle against and mastery over nature, imported from the West, will succeed in competition with ancient and indigenous belief, because the traditional ideas and modern ecological concepts (despite their radically different origins and foundations) have a common foundation in a philosophy of interrelationships. In no respect is the radical change in the Chinese concept of the man-nature relationship more apparent than when it is contrasted, as Murphey does, with the traditional attitudes which have been so great a part, so great a force, in the history of China, for it would be impossible to write an adequate historical geography of that country without considering all these attitudes, *feng-shui* possibly foremost among them.

The concept of man against nature as a philosophy has lost whatever creative force it had in the past. Over the last 100 years the ideas of ecological interrelationships, of the web of life put forward by Darwin, of the biocenose of Möbius, the student of the oyster beds of Sylt, and of the contemporary ecosystem concept have been growing to challenge the traditional dichotomies such as man and nature, man versus nature, man against nature, man's control over nature, or progress as a divorcement from nature.

It is time to take what is creative in both ideas. Today, the idea of an ecosystem is the most acceptable construct that we have for envisaging the organization of nature. It is widely accepted as being fundamental to an understanding of world population growth, the effects of technological innovation, conservation, pollution, and nature protection. But one part of the idea of the man-nature dichotomy as it has developed historically should not be ignored, because it poses squarely the problem of the difference between human and other forms of life, especially as doers, as participating agents in their environment.

In the past, brave attempts have been made to clarify the uniqueness of man and they continue but, unless I am grossly misinformed, we have not gone much beyond the first reassuring platitudes. We have no deep knowledge. We need also to have an understanding of the gulf between human and other life forms as it has developed in varying cultural traditions, and the implications of these findings for the preservation of the natural world, for the prevention of extinctions of threatened plants and animals even if human affairs retain—as indeed they inevitably will—a central position in the preoccupation of man.

Man's technological, innovative, conservative, conserving, humane role can be understood much better in an ecological setting than in one of contrast and antithesis. No good will come of reductionism, of denigrating the inspiring achievements and richness of human culture recorded in libraries, art galleries, museums, conservatories, and universities, especially in a tragic era like this. Man's place in nature, a venerable theme, must be the focus of a new synthesis.

For the most part we have no definitive history of the attitudes of our major civilizations toward nature; they are scattered about almost randomly in such repositories as philosophy, theology, poetry, science, and art history. We do not even have a definitive synthesis of this body of thought in Western civilization, nor of comprehensive national syntheses within it—to say nothing of the attitudes of primitive and preliterate civilizations toward nature.

Agglomerations of public and private decision-making bodies are, and no doubt will continue to be, powerful agents in the molding of our environment. Their decisions often are self-centered, utilitarian, or short-term in outlook. A discussion of a philosophy of man and nature or man in nature thus may seem remote, even disembodied, in such a world; but these decision-makers have their critics, eloquent, well informed and busy, and I will not compete with them. I am more worried about the continued force and influence of general ideas in the face of mindless, glacial power.

I hope, therefore, that there is room for humanistic participation in this broad area of ideas—ideas of different cultures and their histories—especially in the education of the young. We who are associated with universities know full well that our students are rebelling against poverty, racism, and war. Also evident is rebellion against blandness and an intense interest in environment because recognition of the importance of interrelationships needs no special apprenticeship. Fundamental to all these questions and interests, I believe, is the attitude toward life—all life—and the environs in which it exists that a culture or a civilization evolves. The genuine concern for the quality of environment, for the preservation of plants, animals, and human beings from extinction, and for the preservation of historical environments and wilderness is a hopeful sign; it mirrors a reaffirmation of life, its fullness, and beauty.

Single ideas, or groups of them, in the past have been remarkable organizing agents—the ideas of man against nature, Marxism, Darwinism, progress are examples—and other ideas will probably be so in the future. That is why attention should be given to their nature and their history. And the situation is particularly important in the man-nature theme because all signs point to an ever-increasing and intensified manipulation of the physical environment, but hopefully one in which the philosophies of interrelationships, rather than of dichotomies, will become increasingly important.

Conceptions of the interrelationship of man and nature historically have included esthetic, religious, philosophical, in addition to scientific components. In other words, they have included values. They have had to deal, especially in a secular world, with questions of man's stewardship of and responsibility, if any, to other forms of being; with anthropocentrism, the problem of extinction of nonhuman life and of human life by advanced civilizations. The concept of man against nature will become more and more unsatisfactory, if civilization survives, because it cannot accommodate the rich cultural variety of attitudes toward nature by the world's people over millennia, which is expressed in their myth, science, religion, art, and philosophy.

If the history of thought teaches us anything about culture and environment, it is the importance of the conceptions which people have of both—whether these conceptions are religious, philosophical, scientific, or utilitarian. It is a poor time in history to have a narrowness of vision and to continue to limit values to ideas of struggle and antithesis. The diversity of world cultures demands much more of us in understanding and imagination.

The Dilemma of the Coastal Wetlands:
Conflict of Local, National, and World Priorities

William A. Niering

> The creeks overflow: a thousand rivulets run
> 'Twixt the roots of the sod, the blades of the marshgrass
> stir;
> Passeth a hurrying sound of wings that westward whirr;
> Passeth, and all is still; and the currents cease to run;
> And the sea and the marsh are one.

In his descriptive poem "The Marshes of Glynn" (which are located along the shoreline of Georgia), Sidney Lanier has beautifully defined the coastal wetlands where, truly, "the sea and the marsh are one." The tidal-marsh estuarine ecosystem should be of vital concern to everyone. An aquatic complex stretching along the Atlantic and Gulf coasts from Maine to Mexico and along the Pacific from California to the Arctic, it seems almost limitless in extent. Actually it is quite limited; it represents something like .00003 percent of the acreage of our entire country!

The Department of the Interior recognizes 20 different kinds of wetlands in the United States. Originally, they comprised some 127 million acres, but now only 70 million acres—about 60 percent—remain.

The coastal wetlands are strategically located, and consequently they are subject to constant conflicts in multiple use. Sixty percent of this nation's population lives in a band 250 miles wide along the Atlantic, Pacific, and Gulf shorelines. Two thirds of the factories producing pesticides, two thirds of those turning

William A. Niering is director of the Connecticut Arboretum and professor of botany at Connecticut College in New London. He has done extensive ecological research in the South Pacific, the greater metropolitan area of New York City, the mountains and deserts of Arizona and California, and the natural areas of Connecticut. An active conservationist, he is a leading researcher on the dynamics of terrestrial and wetland habitats.

out organic chemical products, about 60 percent of those making inorganic chemicals, 50 percent of the petroleum refining plants, and two thirds of the pulp mills are located in the coastal states. Thus, the evidence is impressive that these lowlands along the shore, these estuaries, are becoming places where the pollutants merge and concentrate, often with deleterious effects on terrestrial and aquatic wildlife.

The estuarine zone serves many purposes, among them transportation, harbors, national security, commercial and industrial sites, waste disposal, abiotic and biotic resources, recreation, and natural beauty. So the many competing possibilities for the use of a single limited region are bound to precipitate conflict and an inevitable dilemma. Our only hope of finding a solution is to evaluate this complex potential ecologically and to establish priorities, rather than to continue the past destructive *laissez-faire* operation.

Of the 27 million acres which are important as fish and wildlife habitat in the 27 states sharing the estuarine zone, about 7 percent—close to 570,000 acres—has been eradicated. The greatest deprivation has occurred in California and northeastern Florida. California leads with a loss of 67 percent, or 256,000 acres out of 382,000 acres of estuarine habitat. Between 10 and 15 percent of the true estuarine environment has been wiped out in New York, New Hampshire, Connecticut, and New Jersey. (In the case of Connecticut, 50 percent of the tidal marshes have been obliterated. The destruction continues daily, eating into the remaining 14,000 acres at the rate of about 200 acres every year.)

A biogeological analysis of this tidal-marsh estuarine system as a natural landscape may more easily resolve some conflicting uses and establish some priorities. Those, in turn, may spotlight more sharply the public's concern at the local, state, federal, and international levels.

Tidal marshes such as those on the Connecticut-Rhode Island border, in southern France at the mouth of the Rhone, exemplify estuarine ecosystems characteristic to the temperate zone. In the latter case, much has been filled in, but surviving marshes contain bands of rushes, glasswort, and sea lavender, which are some of the typical salt marsh plants common in temperate regions. The coastal zone of the tropics such as in southern Florida is dominated by mangroves, rather than the temperate zone's salt marsh grasses, and is very productive in wildlife and aquatic resources.

The tidal-marsh estuarine ecosystem is an interface where the water and land meet, and where nutrients tend to concentrate. In our temperate zone it is a place dominated by grasses, primarily the cordgrasses, which can play an extremely important role in the total marsh ecosystem. Basically, the grasses supply one of the major forms of nutrients that make the estuary a rich and productive area. Each year about half of the grasses that fall onto the marsh flat are partly decomposed by bacteria. About three-quarters of a ton of the dead marsh grass in the form of detritus is swept annually from each acre. As a result of this bacterial action, the total protein content of the grass vegetation is actually increased or even doubled. Therefore, the grasses represent one of the most productive units in the estuarine system.

The mud algae represent another facet contributing to the productivity of the estuarine tidal-marsh complex. Diatoms coating the surface sediments of the mud flats serve as the base of the food chain. They are beautifully adapted to their changing environment, carrying on maximum photosynthesis at high tide in the summer and when the tide is out in the winter and the flats are warmed. Diatoms form a tremendously important contribution to the primary producer biomass.

A third aspect of the estuary's productivity is the phytoplankton, the microscopic plants suspended in the water which serve as another major source of food for zooplankton and other aquatic organisms.

These three major components—the grasses, diatoms, and phytoplankton—make the estuarine tidal marsh one of the world's most productive ecosystems, with an output of up to six times more protein than the cornfields of Iowa. To these one must add the macroscopic algae (seaweeds) which decay; their detritus also makes a sizable contribution to the total productivity.

We have to think of this particular ecosystem as a place where nutrients accumulate and are trapped. Studies by Lawrence Pomeroy, a biologist at the University of Georgia, have indicated that there are about 0.1 parts per billion phosphorus above the marsh and about 10 times more below it, which means that most of the phosphorus is not coming from the land but from the marsh complex. In addition to their production, the nutrients are trapped and held within the estuary. During the tidal cycles the lighter fresh water flows over the salt water, and in the vertical mixing which follows the nutrients are retained within the estuarine system.

The nutrients are trapped not only by this physical aspect of the estuary's hydrology, but also by ribbed mussels embedded within the marsh. These abundant bivalves help stabilize the banks of tidal ditches which have been dredged for mosquito control. As the water sweeps over them, each of these organisms can siphon up to four quarts of water per hour. In that process, they accumulate detritus and phytoplankton in such quantities that they often eject some as pseudofeces, providing further enrichment in the estuary. Thus, the ribbed mussel, commonly regarded as an inedible and unimportant species, actually serves as an important mechanism for keeping the fertility of the estuary high.

The estuary serves as a nursery and a spawning ground for many species, particularly the flounder. Here certain fish spend the early stages of their lives. Providing a nutrient-rich medium, the estuary serves as the base of the food chain for the larval stages of many marine forms during this critical part of their life cycle.

The base of the food chain for shellfish and finfish originates in the estuary. It is the energy derived from this system that accounts for the high shellfish and finfish productivity of our coastal waters. However, it is worth noting that the whole shellfish industry in Connecticut has gone downhill, primarily due to marsh destruction and pollution. Through the 1920s the taking of clams annually netted up to $20 million—equivalent to $48 million in today's economy. At the moment, net clamming profits are down to about $1.5 million.

Significantly, 90 percent of our total seafood harvest is dependent in one way or another upon estuarine environment. In 1960 in New England the fleet landed 800 million pounds of fish valued at over $60 million. About 500,000 pounds of that fish were directly dependent upon the marsh. I have already mentioned the shellfish value which has gone downhill because of a complex of factors; but it can be brought up again, especially if the pollution is abated.

The Sport Fisheries Institute has valued a managed estuarine acre off the Maine coast at $33,563. This figure is based on the potential harvest of shellfish and bait worms. Where such acreage is not managed, about one half that value is estimated. By comparison, the market value of a good acre in upland Maine is about $2000.

In various parts of the world, production of shellfish and finfish has greatly increased when estuarine areas are managed. That may be necessary in this country if we hope to help in feeding our world population. With the population doubling every few decades, and with more than half of humanity suffering from malnutrition, it seems to me that on a long-range basis we cannot afford to lose this tidal marsh habitat.

Commercial oystermen are attempting to increase oyster productivity by submerging strings of scallop shells in unpolluted bays where the young oyster spat settle on the shells and grow. Without any special fertilization, it is possible to achieve tremendous quantities of these young spat, which can be eventually seeded in the estuary to mature to marketable size.

The production of wildlife is another important characteristic of the estuaries. The spectacular water birds associated with the marsh attract millions of people annually. The marshes along the east coast are in the path of the Atlantic flyway. Tremendous numbers of birds stop on the marshes to rest and feed during the migration periods. Many also nest. In fact, it is estimated that during an average year 300,000 ducks—and in the best years 700,000—are produced along the eastern coastal wetlands. This particular environment is quite literally a duck factory!

Among the most distinctive birds of the marsh are the rails.

The clapper rail, one of the most common, is a secretive bird seldom seen by the casual marsh visitor. In addition, the spectacular waders, the herons and egrets, are most frequently seen as they search for food along the mud flats at low tide.

Because of its declining numbers, the osprey has excited most attention at this particular moment. Studies by Peter Ames, University of California ornithologist, have documented a correlation between the amount of DDT found in the eggs of the osprey and their hatchability. In the Connecticut eggs he found that it took two nests to produce one offspring, while there was one bird per nest in Maryland. Checking the DDT content, he discovered about five parts per million in the Connecticut eggs and only three parts per million in those from Maryland. In simple terms: less DDT in the Maryland eggs and a little bit better hatchability, more DDT in the Connecticut eggs and poorer hatchability. Normally, one can expect two or more young ospreys to hatch per nest.

Although only a correlation, Ames' findings stimulated the examination of some other factors. Lucille Stickel, at the U.S. Department of the Interior's Patuxent Research Center, correlated differential eggshell thickness in pesticide-fed birds. Mallard ducks particularly, which were fed DDT in their diets, produced eggs with shells measuring 13 percent thinner than those produced by birds that had not been fed the pesticide. Joseph Hickey, wildlife biologist at the University of Wisconsin, analyzed the eggshell thickness of hawk eggs from various museums, collected before 1945, and compared them with more recent eggs of the same species. Here his correlation indicated a 19 percent decrease in the thickness of the eggshell, which means increased breakage in the nest and fewer birds hatched. Hickey also found that the change in the thickness of the eggs occurred about 1947. This correlation is significant because we began to use persistent pesticides at about that time. This adds further evidence regarding the role of pesticides in the declining population of our birds of prey.

Back from the edge of the estuary where the water is slightly brackish, extensive cattail marshes provide refuge for the redwing blackbird, an interesting bird with a fascinating social behavior. Extensive studies have been carried out on this particular bird, which in many areas causes considerable damage to agricultural crops. One of the control measures has been the use of detergents on these birds in an effort to disperse them. To understand this species better, Richard S. Miller, Oastler Professor of Wildlife Ecology at Yale, and Gordon Orians, University of Washington biologist, are studying the birds' social behavior and life history. The knowledge which they—and others like them—might gain by saving these wetland areas could conceivably prove to be so fundamental that improved control measures could be applied to agricultural trouble spots throughout the nation.

A congressman recently questioned the validity of providing funds for research on redwing blackbirds. In reply, Orians submitted an excellent commentary which pointed out that he is preparing a book on the whole problem of man's social organization and population stress; much of his information is coming from insights gained in his studies of redwing blackbirds!

A considerable number of animals such as deer and raccoon, typically found in upland sites, are also dependent upon the marsh, which has an intricate role in providing a diversity of food typically associated with their diet.

A third important aspect concerning the marsh is its rather unique vegetational pattern. The combination of salinity, changing tides, and periodic storms which hit the estuaries builds up striking vegetational patterns. Bands of different vegetation result from the complex of interacting factors. They range from three- to five-foot-high switch grass on through black grass *(Juncus gerardi),* salt meadow cordgrass *(Spartina patens),* and salt marsh cordgrass *(Spartina alternifolia)* typically bordering the tidal ditches and creeks. Depressions within this banding pattern result in a diversity of colorful forms such as sea lavender, gerardia, and glasswort.

The geologic role played by the marshes cannot be ignored. Their actual buildup is a fascinating process, particularly as described by Alfred Redfield in his reconstruction of the ontogeny of marsh development over the past 4000 years on Cape Cod marsh.[1]

First the silt or clay is laid down, then the peat of tall salt-water grass which is constantly flooded because it is very low marsh. The peat builds up to several feet and finally reaches a point where the *Spartina patens* or salt meadow cordgrass is able to take root. Such a 4000-year developmental process can be destroyed by man in a single day. It has happened all too frequently.

However, it seems to me that these marshes play a most significant geologic role as sediment accretors. A study by Yale geologists Sanders and Ellis[2] has indicated that those sediments which do not form the marsh complex go instead into channels, harbors, or tidal creeks, accentuating problems of silting. Tidal marshes also serve as a coastal buffer. During severe storms these extensive mats of marsh peat exhibit great resilience, providing the upland with an added degree of protection.

From the standpoint of further research an interesting coastal submergence problem occurs in the marsh. The major rise in sea level was probably accomplished about 5000 years ago from the melting of glacial ice, but it is still increasing about three inches a century. This means that the coastal marsh is still encroaching on the upland. By preserving valley marshes exhibiting the total spectrum of species from saline to fresh water one can document how this dynamic process affects the vegetational pattern and associated underlying sediments.

Now that we have examined the various roles of the tidal marshes, let us consider some of the conflicts concerning them. An obvious conflict occurs over the encroachment of filling, which reminds me of Shakespeare's statement that "when you take my life, you take the place in which I dwell." A classic example in Connecticut was the creation of a parking lot by

[1] *Estuaries,* ed. George H. Lauff (Washington, American Association for the Advancement of Science, 1967).

[2] John E. Sanders and Charles W. Ellis, "Geological Aspects of Connecticut's Coastal Marshes," in *Connecticut's Coastal Marshes—A Vanishing Resource,* Connecticut Arboretum Bulletin no. 12 (1961).

marsh filling at Sherwood Island State Park. Dredging for the installation of a marina is another case in point. Although more marinas may be needed they need not be located in a tidal marsh.

A second conflict: are we going to have marshes for ducks, or are we going to have them for the production of finfish and shellfish? These marshes can be impounded and converted to fresh-water areas. They are unquestionably able to produce more ducks, but certain of their other productivity qualities are lost. Other disturbances include the blasting of holes into the marsh in duck management programs.

Agricultural pollution can also be a problem. A survey has found that the duck farms at Moriches Bay on Long Island contributed tremendously to the transformation of the bay's whole phytoplankton population. Instead of the normal diatom population of many different species, the result was two species of chlorophyllaceous algae which were not beneficial to oysters. The bay's ecology had actually been changed by a particular enrichment with organic matter. Laboratory tests indicated that these two species of algae were favored by the organic nitrogen available in such tremendous quantities.

How do we resolve the conflicts that imperil our estuarine marshes? We will continue to need navigation, transportation, and harbors along the nation's coastline. Obviously, oil discharges, whether from ships or underwater wells, show the necessity for more stringent regulation. Also essential is sewage control from ships, industry, and agriculture, and even domestic sources.

The cleanup process will be long and costly. It could start with strict rules and enforcement for vessels, and then similar provisions for pulp mills where effluents deplete the estuarine waters of oxygen. Oysters there have been found to be 500 times more sensitive to the effluent than fish. Or the cleanup campaign could aim at another critical problem, chemical wastes where Pacific salmon move through the estuary. Many aquatic and terrestrial organisms are extremely sensitive to metals such as cobalt, copper, and mercury which are being flushed into the water flowing into the sea. Again, it is obvious that new and stricter regulations on effluents are required.

Agricultural chemicals create a more difficult problem. How can we prevent leaching of pesticides off the landscape into surrounding estuaries? The lower Mississippi fish kill in 1963 was a dramatic example where extensive numbers of catfish were killed by the pesticide endrin. A chemical company was largely responsible, but some of the insecticide presumably came from surrounding agricultural lands.

Control of materials that get into the estuary is complex and difficult but must be governed from the source where possible. Oysters not only are sensitive to insecticides but can accumulate great quantities of them—in one experiment up to 70,000 times the average amount in the surrounding water. This is the problem of biological magnification. Even if the pesticide content entering a stream is relatively low, animals such as the bivalves become accumulators of the deadly material.

Obviously, we need more than new regulations and enforcement. The treatment of our addiction to pesticides requires an entirely new approach, integrated biological control systems with pesticides serving as only part of the total design. Various cultural techniques can be employed. In the case of cotton in California, scientists learned that by planting alternate rows of alfalfa they have been able to divert some insects from the cotton to the alfalfa. We must expand our search for such integrated control techniques so that only minimal amounts of pesticides are necessary. It will cost a lot of money and require government subsidy. Marketing inspectors and consumers must modify their demands for insect-free produce. High-powered advertising has accustomed us to the idea that every commodity must be virtually perfect; this is not necessary.

Thermal heating is another industrial conflict in the estuarine environment. Senator Edmund Muskie of Maine criticized the Atomic Energy Commission in 1968 when it failed to consider thermal heating, in addition to radioactive contamination, as its problem. Muskie's reflections have also alerted some utilities to be more careful. Daniel Merriman of Yale University has been carrying on studies at the Connecticut Yankee nuclear energy plant on the effects of thermal heating, and Nelson Marshall at the Rhode Island Oceanographic Institute has started long-range research at the plant under construction at Millstone Point. These experts and others are attempting, as the AEC has done for many years in the case of radioactivity, to determine the ecological changes likely to evolve from nuclear power plant operations.

A utility executive recently said that the demand for electricity will double in the next ten years. Actually, the estimates range from 32 to 512-fold by the year 2000. That will put a tremendous demand on the utility systems. It also will pose a rather interesting ethical point: do we really need all the electricity utility companies plan to try to sell us? The question may encroach a little on the free enterprise system concept, but remember that we are all on this planet together. Conceivably, sooner or later we will face the choice of sacrificing some electricity or certain estuarine ecosystems.

Domestic pollution is a serious threat to our environmental welfare. Our rivers are so polluted that we cannot swim in them. The Thames River flows by my house here in Connecticut. It looks beautiful from the distance, but I cannot swim in it and certainly do not want to fish in it. Millions of gallons of sewage come daily into the Thames from the cities of Norwich and Taftville. Of course, this problem will be solved soon if the federal and state governments can match enough funds. But funds are in short supply and the pollution is increasing.

There is no doubt that we recognize the crisis. Appropriate legislation has been passed in an attempt to clean up the nation's water, but it will take some time. In fact, it is going to take quite a bit of time, because so much of our tax money is being diverted to other uses. In the first year after the Clean Water Restoration Act was passed in 1966 the demand from cities for matching federal funds far outstripped the money available. It all boils down to getting enough financial aid to help cities clean up first, so that the estuarine environment can be salvaged too.

Another conflict centers on our abiotic resources. This, basically, involves the taking of sand and gravel from beneath estuaries for such purposes as construction of the Connecticut Thruway or parking facilities on the marsh at the Sherwood Island

State Park. That resource below the estuary is immensely valuable, and some shrewd businessmen with their eyes on it have approached the Connecticut Resources Commission several times to suggest a rather interesting kind of dredging ditch—one which would serve only a single purpose, to get at the sand and gravel deposits. Such a venture was undertaken in Florida with the predictable result that after ten years of dredging an estuary, very little bottom fauna remains. The removal of such a resource is wanton, unforgivable destruction.

Mining oil on the coastal shelf can create problems. The incidents of the leaking oil wells off Santa Barbara, California, speak for themselves as a potential future threat to the biota of the coastal zone.

Another threat to our existing marshes is filling in conjunction with recreational development. In the recently acquired Bluff Point State Park in Groton, Connecticut, the initial plans proposed the filling of about one third of the wetlands, leaving what somebody has designated as the "valuable wetlands." However, no one has demonstrated that the ill-fated one third of the wetlands is not valuable; until such proof is offered I would suggest that we leave it inviolate. In my opinion, it does not have to be filled, because there are alternate ways which we have not yet even considered for getting people to shoreline parks. For instance, if they have driven a long distance, they might enjoy a boat ride as the last lap of their jaunt to the park. Or how about busing the swimmers from a nearby inland parking area, rather than filling in the wetlands so they can put their cars on the former marsh? Nobody has really explored all of the alternatives available in trying to preserve this invaluable resource, but the need is critical.

At the global level, the International Union for the Protection of Nature held a conference in the early 60s in an attempt to stimulate the preservation of wetlands on an international scale. Many constructive resolutions were passed. At the federal level we have a Water Pollution Control Administration, and a Clean Water Act. A national survey is also underway to inventory and evaluate estuaries, and to make recommendations on what should be preserved.

Two bills are pending in the Connecticut General Assembly. [Since the presentation of this paper a Connecticut Wetlands Bill was passed in the 1969 legislature.] They would provide good wetlands legislation similar to that already in effect in Massachusetts, Rhode Island, and Maine.

The land trusts, of which 12 are already established in Connecticut, make up another—and one of the finest—methods of generating local interest and getting action started from the ground level.

I strongly recommend that we declare a moratorium on any further destruction of wetland resources until all have been inventoried and ecologically evaluated. Then we should develop a national wetlands policy in cooperation with other countries.

This responsibility cannot be delegated to state and local governments; it must begin at the federal level, because the marshes and estuaries cross political boundaries. Our system has proved to be archaic at resolving some of these situations. All kinds of conflicts, not only at the state and local levels, but even at the federal level, have developed because we lack a wetlands policy. The Army Corps of Engineers has fought with the Department of the Interior over problems concerning the Everglades. We have seen one federal agency try to preserve wetlands for ducks, while another wants to fill them for agriculture. We have even seen the Department of Commerce making grants to communities to study the feasibility of using coastal wetlands as locations for developments to stimulate the local economy. It is clearly evident that there is no national wetlands policy.

We need broadly trained advisers who can examine the total ecological system, rather than people just looking at the problems of ducks or food production. This opinion has been supported by a recent Harvard study under IBM sponsorship on "The Impact of Technology on Society."[3] The researchers found that the im-

[3] Emmanuel G. Mesthene, "The Impact of Technology on Society," Fourth annual report of the Harvard University Program on Technology and Society (1969).

pact has provided the individual with a greater sense of worth (a questionable conclusion.) It was also evident from their discussion that our affluence has resulted in many effluents.

One of the difficulties with modern technology has been that the profit-making corporation is not yet entirely geared to deal with social problems or pollution. Another is that it has not been anyone's business to look at this problem. The consequence has been unrestrained technological individualism, much like the unbridled economic individualism of the pre-New Deal days. This is why I recommend that a broader group start looking at the big, the total, ecological picture.

In summary, a statement by Senator Henry M. Jackson in *Bioscience* (December 1967), pointedly touches at the heart of the issue. Senator Jackson said:

> In the future we must strive to improve the methods of economic analysis by which environmental management decisions are made. We must recognize that the marketplace often deals in illusions, that much of the profit of yesterday turns out today to be shortsighted because the price tag did not include all the social and economic costs.

Fun and Games with the Gross National Product— The Role of Misleading Indicators in Social Policy

Kenneth E. Boulding

The Gross National Product is one of the great inventions of the twentieth century, probably almost as significant as the automobile and not quite so significant as TV. The effect of *physical* inventions is obvious, but social inventions like the GNP change the world almost as much.

The idea of the total product of society is fairly old, certainly dating back to Adam Smith, but the product's measurement is very much a matter of the second half of the 1900s, which I suppose we can call the fortieth half-century. Before 1929 we did not really have any adequate measure of the Gross National Product, although its measurement was pioneered by Simon Kuznets and others at the National Bureau of Economic Research from 1919 on. We began to get theories which used it in the '30s, and the cumulative effect has been substantial.

Every science must develop its own Tycho Brahe, the sixteenth century Danish gentleman who painstakingly plotted the planets' positions and thus paved the way for Johannes Kepler and Isaac Newton. In a way, Wesley Mitchell was the Tycho Brahe of economics. He painstakingly collected time series of economic quantities, although (like Tycho Brahe) he was operating with a largely erroneous theory. However, the studies at Mitchell's National Bureau of Economic Research led to the invention of the Gross National Product as a measure, and this has had an enormous effect on economic policy.

Kenneth E. Boulding is professor of economics and directs the program on General Social and Economic Dynamics at the Institute of Behavioral Science, University of Colorado. He has been president of the American Economic Association and the Society for General Systems Research, and is a fellow of the American Academy of Arts and Sciences and of the American Philosophical Society. He is the author of many books on economic theory and principles.

It is hard to underestimate the impact of economic measures on the world. A good example of a rather deplorable measure was the parity index, which had a tremendous impact on our agricultural policy—especially in the 1930s and '40s. The Bureau of Agricultural Economics in the Department of Agriculture developed indexes for the prices paid by farmers and for the prices received by farmers; then some enthusiast divided one by the other and came up with the parity index, which is a measure of the terms of trade of agriculture. This then became an ideal.

The danger of measures is precisely that they become ideals. You see it even in the thermostat. If we had no Fahrenheit, we would not be stabilizing our room temperature too high. There is a magic about the number 70, and we tend to stabilize the temperature at it, when for the sake of health it might be better at 64 degrees. Certainly, one should never underestimate the power of magic numbers. We are really all Pythagoreans. Once we get a number, we sit down and worship it.

The parity ideal was a mistake, but it proved to be astonishingly successful. I do not want to get into this because it is another subject, but one of these days after I retire I want to write a history of the United States on the principle that we always have done the right thing for the wrong reasons. Our agricultural policy for the last 30 years is a prize example of this. Parity was sold to the people and to Congress under the name of social justice. The measure of social justice was the parity index, which was an index of terms of trade of agriculture with 1909-14 as a base.

Well, how stupid can we get? There is nothing sacred about terms of trade if the differential rates of productivity change, and they have changed. You do not establish social justice at all by stabilizing terms of trade. Terms of trade of progressive industries often worsen, as in agriculture; the terms of trade of stagnant industries like education ought to get better, as they have done. Educators today are richer, not because *they* are more productive (which they are not) but because *other people* are more productive. As education's terms of trade have improved substantially, the unit cost of education has correspondingly risen.

Incidentally, when we tried to establish social justice with "parity," which meant, of course, that we raised agricultural prices, we subsidized the rich farmers and penalized the poor. If you try to establish social justice through the price system, you always benefit the rich because the rich have more to start with. Agricultural poverty is always the result of people having not very much to buy and sell. If you do not have anything to buy and sell, it does not matter what prices you do not buy and sell it at. So manipulation of prices—whether of agricultural policy or of cheap education—always succeeds in subsidizing the rich in the same way that state universities subsidize the rich.

All of this may seem to be a long way from the GNP. Actually, I am trying to illustrate this: when you measure something, you inevitably affect people's behavior; and as a measure of the total gross output of the economy, the GNP has had an enormous impact on behavior.

A fascinating book, *The Fiscal Revolution in America* (University of Chicago Press, 1969), has been written by Herbert Stein. He is a member of the Council of Economic Advisers who are the Three Wise Men in our society, the bishops of the modern world, Congress having established an economic episcopate. Stein has done an extremely interesting study, an intellectual history explaining the great change in economic policy from the administration of Herbert Hoover to that of John F. Kennedy.

In the depths of the depression, Hoover engineered a tax increase which exacerbated the depression. That dark hour in the global economy contributed to the rise of Adolf Hitler who precipitated World War II. Had it not been for all those developments we might not have had today's Russian problem; we might not even have had Vietnam. Hoover never knew what hit him because he did not have a Council of Economic Advisers. We did not know much economics in those days. We did not know about the GNP.

Kennedy, in a much milder situation, fostered a tax cut which was an enormous success. As a result, we have had the bloated '60s, the decade without a depression. That should go down in the history books as something spectacular. It is the longest boom ever enjoyed in the United States. Economics has had something to do with it. So has the GNP.

These days, if the GNP starts to go down, an economic adviser will go to the President and say, "Oh, look, Mr. Nixon. The GNP dropped half a point. We have to do something about this." This is the beauty of having social cybernetics, an information system that we can use to our advantage.

I suspect that without economics we might have had a Great Depression in the 1950s and '60s. The rate of return on investment in economics may be at least 10,000 percent per annum, because we have not put much into it and we have gotten a lot out of it. On the other hand, this very success worries me. I have revised some folk wisdom lately; one of my edited proverbs is "Nothing fails like success," because you do not learn anything from it. The only thing we ever learn from is failure. Success only confirms our superstitions.

For some strange reason which I do not understand at all a small subculture arose in western Europe which legitimated failure. Science is the only subculture in which failure is legitimate. When astronomers Albert A. Michelson and Edward W. Morley did an experiment which proved to be a dud (in some eyes), they did not just bury it the way the State Department does. Instead, they shouted the results from the housetops, and revised the whole image of the universe. In political life—and to a certain extent in family life—when we make an Edsel, we bury it. We do not learn from our mistakes. Only in the scientific community is failure legitimated. The very success of the GNP and the success of economics should therefore constitute a solemn warning.

I am something of an ecologist at heart, mainly because I am really a preacher, and we know that all ecologists are really preachers under the skin. They are great viewers with alarm. Is there any more single-minded, simple pleasure than viewing with alarm? At times it is even better than sex.

I propose, then, to view the GNP with alarm.

The Gross National Product is supposed to be a measure of economic success, or economic welfare, or something like that. Of course, it is not. So we have to modify it.

In the first place, the Gross National Product is too gross. It includes a number of things which should be netted out. If we are going to get the net benefit of our economic activity, we have to net the national product, and the real question is how net can we make it? We get first what we call the Net National Product, which technically is the Gross National Product minus depreciation.

The GNP is like the Red Queen in *Alice Through the Looking Glass:* it runs as fast as it can to stay where it is. It includes all the depreciation of capital, so we net that out.

We really ought to net out all sorts of other things such as the military, which is also in the GNP and does not produce much. The world war industry is really a self-contained exercise in mutual masochism. The war industry of each country depends on the other's war industry, and it is a largely self-contained system. It has little to do with defense. It is extremely expensive and very dangerous, and we certainly ought to net it out of the product. That takes out about 10 percent.

Things like commuting and pollution also should be netted out. When somebody pollutes something and somebody else cleans it up, the cleanup is added to the national product and the pollution is not subtracted; that, of course, is ridiculous. In fact, I have been conducting a mild campaign to call the GNP the Gross National Cost rather than the product. It really represents what we have to produce, first to stay where we are and second to get a little farther along.

I have been arguing for years (and nobody has paid the slightest attention) that the real measure of economic welfare is not income at all. It is the state or condition of the person, or of the society. Income is just the unfortunate price that we have to pay because the state is corruptible. We have breakfast, and breakfast depreciates; so we must have lunch. The sole reason for lunch is metabolism, and metabolism is decay. Most change is truly decay. Consumption is decay—your automobile wearing out, your clothes becoming threadbare. It is burning up the gasoline. It is eating up the food. Consumption is a bad, not a good thing; production is what we must undergo because of consumption.

Things will not stay as they are because of a reality which I sometimes call the Law of Moth and Rust. What causes our illusion that welfare is measured by the Gross National Product or anything else related to income (that is, any flow variable)? The more there is, the more is consumed; therefore, the more we must produce to replace what has been consumed. The bigger the capital stock, the more it will be consumed; hence, the more you have to produce to replace it and, of course, add to it if you want to increase it. In this sense the GNP has a kind of rough relationship with the stock or state, but I think it should always be regarded as a cost rather than a product.

Another minor item, perhaps just a technical point: as we measure it, the GNP neglects household production and only includes items in the market. If a man marries his housekeeper, the GNP falls; I argue that if he was a moral man the GNP ought to rise because he is enjoying all he had before and then some. Obviously, there is a small technical defect. However, household production probably is not much more than 5 percent, certainly not more than 10 percent, of the GNP, and thus it is a minor issue.

Much more fundamental is that all of economics, the whole GNP mentality, assumes that economic activity is a throughput, a linear process from the mine to the garbage dump.

The ultimate physical product of economic life is garbage. The system takes ores and fossil fuels (and in a boom the unemployed) out of the earth, chews them up in the process of production, and eventually spews them out into sewers and garbage dumps. We manage to have state or condition in the middle of the throughput in which we are well fed and well clothed, in which we can travel, in which we have buildings in which we are protected from the atrocious climate and enabled to live in the temperate zone. Just imagine how the GNP would fall and welfare would rise if man abandoned the temperate zone and moved into the tropics. An enormous amount of the GNP is heating this building because the plain truth is that nature is very disagreeable. It is cold, damp, and miserable, and the main effort of human activity is to get away from it. As a matter of fact, we do not even like pure air. Otherwise we would not smoke. All of this indicates that a great deal of man's activity is directed toward what we might call desired pollution.

The throughput is going to come to an end. We are approaching the end of an era. People have been saying it for a long time, but nobody has ever believed them. Very often they were wrong in their forecasts, but this time I suspect they are right. We really are approaching the end of the era of expanding man.

Up to now, man has psychologically lived on a flat earth—a great plain, in fact a "darkling plain" where "ignorant armies clash by night," as Matthew Arnold says. Man has always had somewhere to go. There has always been a Kansas somewhere to beckon him as a virgin land of promise. There is no longer any Kansas. The photographs of the earth by astronauts in lunar orbit symbolize the end of this era. Clearly the earth is a beautiful little spaceship, all blue and green and white, with baroque cloud patterns on it, and its destination unknown. It is getting pretty crowded and its resources rather limited.

The problem of the present age is that of the transition from the Great Plains into the spaceship or into what Barbara Ward and I have been calling spaceship earth. We do not have any mines and we do not have any sewers in a spaceship. The water has to go through the algae to the kidneys to the algae to the kidneys, and so on, and around and around and around. If the earth is to become a spaceship, we must develop a cyclical economy within which man can maintain an agreeable state.

Under such circumstances the idea of the GNP simply falls apart. We need a completely different set of concepts for that eventuality, and we are still a long way from it technologically because we never had to worry about it. We always have had an unlimited Schmoo, Al Capp's delightful cartoon creature that everlastingly gets its kicks from being the main course for gluttonous man. We could just rip the earth apart and sock it away. We used to think Lake Erie was a great lake; now it smells like the Great Society. We used to think the oceans were pretty big, but events like the oil leakage in California have spotlighted that fallacy. Suddenly, it is becoming obvious that the Great Plain has come to an end and that we are in a very crowded spaceship. This is a fundamental change in human consciousness, and it will require an adjustment of our ethical, religious, and national systems which may be quite traumatic.

On the whole, human society has evolved in response to a fairly unlimited environment. That is not true of all societies, of course. It is not so true of the Indian village, but the societies that are mainly cyclical are almost uniformly disagreeable. Even the societies which are cyclical (where you return the night soil to the farms) are not really circular. They rely on water and solar energy coming down from somewhere and going out to somewhere. There is some sort of an input-output.

Up to now we have not even begun to solve the problem of a high-level circular economy. In fact, we have not even been interested in it. We did not have to be, because it was so far off in the future. Now it is still a fair way off. Resources for the Future says, "We're all right, Jack. We've got a hundred years." Its report points to our fossil fuels and our ores, and reassures us that they will be adequate for a century. After that, the deluge. I would not be a bit surprised if we run out of pollutable reservoirs before our mines and ores are exhausted. There are some signs of this happening in the atmosphere, in the rivers, and in the oceans.

The nitrogen cycle, the extraction of nitrogen from the air, exemplifies the development of what looks like the beginning of a spaceship technology. Surely, when man looks back on the twentieth century, he will regard the development of the Haber process in 1913 as its most important event, even though it did permit World War I. If it had not been for Fritz Haber, the Germans would not have been able to fight that war because they were cut off from Chilean nitrates. Historically, there was a famous viewer-with-alarm about 1899, the English chemist Sir William Crookes, who predicted the exhaustion of Chile's nitrates and consequent global starvation by 1930. His prophecy did not pan out, thanks to the Haber process.

That process was the beginning of an anti-entropic process of production, entropic in the sense of material entropy. We need a word for this, and it does not exist. Ordinary economic processes diffuse the concentrated. We start off with concentrations of ores and fuels, and we spread them over the earth into dumps or into oceans. This is entropic in the sense of returning to chaos. The Haber process concentrated the diffuse; it showed that if you put energy into the system, you could reverse the material entropy.

That is an old trick. It is called life, and it was invented a long time ago. However, Haber's process marked the first time that any living organism had invented a new formula for it. Without Haber we would certainly be in much worse shape than we are today. We would have had mass famine in this century, without question. Barry Commoner, Professor of Plant Physiology at Washington University, says that in the Middle West, for instance, we are now dumping into the cycle about twice the amount of nitrogen we used in the days before artificial fertilizers were developed. This means that nearly all the rivers in Illinois are now eutrophic, and where will it all lead?

Can we overload the nitrogen cycle without creating extremely alarming ecological consequences? That is something we shall have to answer. My IBM spies tell me that a fundamental doctrine applied to computers is called the Gigo Principle, standing for "garbage in, garbage out." It is a basic law that what you put in you have to take out. This is throughput. Otherwise, we have to recycle everything, and we have not begun to consider the problems of a high-level, recycled economy. I am pretty sure there is no nonexistence theorem about it. I am certain that a recycling technology is possible which, of course, must have an input of energy. Nobody is going to repeal the second law of thermodynamics, not even the Democrats. This means that if we are to avoid the increase of material entropy, we must have an input of energy into the system. The present system has an enormous input of energy in fossil fuels which cannot last very long unless we go to nuclear fusion. In that case there is an awful lot of water around, and it would last a long time.

Fission is not any good; it is just messy. I understand that if we began using uranium to produce all our power requirements in this country, we would run out of it in ten years. So actually nuclear energy is not a great source of energy; this planet's coal probably has more. Nuclear energy is not a great new field opened up. I suspect it could turn out to be rather dangerous nonsense.

What does this leave us with? The good old sun. At the most pessimistic, you might say we have to devise a basic economy which relies on the input of solar energy for all its energy requirements. As we know, there is a lot of solar energy.

On the other hand, what we do not know is how many people this spaceship earth will support at a high level. We do not know this even to order of magnitude. I suggest that this is one of the major research projects for the next generation, because the whole future of man depends on it. If the optimum population figure is 100 million, we are in for a rough time. It could be as low as that if we are to have a really high-level economy in which everything is recycled. Or it could be up to 10 billion. If it is up to 10 billion, we are okay, Jack—at least for the time being. A figure somewhere between 100 million and 10 billion is a pretty large area of ignorance. I have a very uneasy feeling that it may be towards the lower level, but we do not really know that.

We do not really know the limiting factor. I think we can demonstrate, for instance, that in all probability the presently underdeveloped countries are not going to develop. There is not enough of anything. There is not enough copper. There is not enough of an enormous number of elements which are essential to the developed economy. If the whole world developed to American standards overnight, we would run out of everything in less than 100 years.

Economic development is the process by which the evil day is brought closer when everything will be gone. It will result in final catastrophe unless we treat this interval in the history of man as an opportunity to make the transition to the spaceship earth.

Now that I have been rude to the Gross National Product, let me show how it *can* be used and the things it suggests. In an interesting little empirical trick (it is not much more than that) I have plotted the *GNP per capita,* which is a very rough measure of how rich a country is already, against the logarithm of the *rate of growth* of GNP per capita for all the countries where information was available. Despite the measure's defects, I think that the data are meaningful.

The GNP per capita varies from about $50 for Haiti to more than $3000 for the United States; when the range is that much it must mean something—even if you do not know what. The yearly rate of growth per capita ranges from about 10 percent in Japan to minus 2 percent for Uruguay in the first half of the 1960s.

The countries of the world then divide clearly into two groups. One, which I call the A countries, includes Japan, the USSR, Yugoslavia, Hungary, Belgium, Italy, Denmark, and, indeed, most of the countries of the temperate zone; they lie along a downward-sloping straight line, with Japan at the top and the United States at the bottom. In this group the richer you are, the slower you grow. This is a fundamental law of growth and, so far as I know, all natural growth systems obey such a rule. Certainly, exponential growth of anything never goes on for very long. If it ever did, it would be the only thing in the universe. Obviously, there is a nonexistence theorem about exponential growth. The A countries exhibit logistic growth, or at least the appearance of it.

The other group, the B countries, are all in the tropics with some exceptions, mainly in Latin America. They occupy a circular area in the bottom left-hand corner of the figure. They do not seem to be going anywhere, but they have sort of a Brownian movement. Their rates of growth are far below countries of equal poverty in the A group. This suggests that the developmental process has a "main line." If you are on this line, you will go on getting richer; but as you get richer, you get rich more slowly—which is not surprising. If this goes on for a century, all the A countries will begin to slide down the line to the bottom, and will be equally rich and equally slow. In the meantime, unless some of the B countries get on the main line they are not going anywhere.

This is the most significant example I have found to illustrate the use of the GNP as a measure of some kind of process. Consequently, I am not prepared to ditch the GNP altogether. It is a measure of some process in the United States that took us from about $100 per capita at the time of the Revolution to $3000 today. It is a real process, and the difference between Haiti and the United States is very real. We are rich and they are poor; no question about it. This is mainly a result of the development process, not of exploitation. The one thing it suggests is that exploitation is a minor element in explaining the differences of wealth in the world. If some countries are rich and some are poor, it is because the rich countries are on the main line of development, or have been on it longer, and the poor countries are not. The reason for the United States' wealth today is that we have had fairly consistent economic growth for well over 150 years.

The American Revolution cost a generation of growth, as all revolutions do, whether they are one-generation revolutions like ours or two-generation revolutions like that of the Soviet Union. Revolutions always set nations back, although they may start off the process of growth. We recovered from the Boston Tea Party by about 1815, and then we took off. From that point on, we approximately doubled the per capita income every generation. If you do that, you go 100, 200, 400, 800, 1600, 3200. It takes six generations that way. On the whole, this has been the rate of development before World War II.

Now the Japanese GNP is growing at 8 to 10 percent per capita per annum, which is absurd. This means that in Japan the children are six times as rich as their parents, which I think is greedy. I am quite happy with a 4 percent rise, which makes the children twice as rich as the parents, as in the United States. In the same 150 years India (or Haiti even worse) has gone 100, 100, 100, 100, 100. Or perhaps 100, 110, 120, 90, or something like that. It is the difference in the rate of development which explains the difference in per capita GNP.

On the other hand, this kind of process does not at all answer the question that I raised in the first half of this discussion. When we get to $10,000 per capita, what does it really mean? Does it simply mean that we are exhausting the resources of the earth at a much more rapid rate? Of course, we have a process here of increased efficiency in exploitation of the earth, not exploitation of man. We go on, we become terribly rich, and suddenly it is all gone. We may have a process of this sort.

What may happen is that we are going to have to face something of this sort in the next 500 years. Unquestionably, we will have to aim for much lower levels of growth, because the cyclical process costs more than the throughput does. However, if we devote our knowledge industries to solution of the problem of the cyclical economy, maybe it will turn out all right.

The idea that we are moving into a world of absolutely secure and effortless abundance is nonsense. This is an illusion of the young who are supported by their parents. Once they have children of their own, they realize that abundance is an illusion. It is a plausible illusion, because we have had an extraordinary two centuries. We have had an extraordinary period of economic growth and of the discovery of new resources.

But this is not a process that can go on forever, and we do not know how abundant this spaceship is going to be. Nobody here now is going to live to see the spaceship, because it is certainly 100 years—perhaps 500 years—off. I am sure it will be no longer than 500 years off, and that is not a tremendously long period of historic time.

An extraordinary conference was held last December [1968] on the Ecological Consequences of International Development. It was an antidevelopment gathering of ecologists, who presented 60 developmental horror stories, among them predictions that the Aswan Dam is going to ruin Egypt, the Kariba Dam will ruin central Africa, DDT will ruin us all, insecticides will ruin the cotton crops, thallium will ruin Israel, and so on all down the line. Some of these forecasts I take with a little grain of ecological salt. The cumulative effect, however, is significant, and suggests that no engineer should be allowed into the world without an ecologist in attendance as a priest. The most dangerous thing in the world is the completely untrammeled engineer. A friend of mine was at the Aswan Dam talking to the Russian engineer in charge. He asked him about all the awful ecological consequences: snails, erosion, evaporation, and such. The engineer replied, "Well, that is not my business. My job is just to build the dam."

We are all like that, really. I have recently discovered the real name of the devil, which is something terribly important to know. The real name of the devil is *suboptimization,* finding out the best way to do something which should not be done at all. The engineers, the military, the governments, and the corporations are all quite busy at this. Even professors try to find the best way of giving a Ph.D. degree, which to my mind should not be done at all. We are all suboptimizers.

The problem of how to prevent suboptimization is, I think, the great problem of social organization. The only people who have thought about it are the economists, and they have the wrong answer, which was perfect competition. Nobody else has any answer at all. Obviously, the deep, crucial problem of social organization is how to prevent people from doing their best when the best in the particular, in the small, is not the best in the large.

The answer to this problem lies mainly in the ecological point of view, which is perhaps the most fundamental thing we can teach anybody. I am quite sure that it has to become the basis of our educational system.

I have added a verse to a long poem I wrote at that ecological conference. There are some who may still shrug off its somber tone, but the wise man—and nation—will take heed.

> With development extended to the whole of planet earth
> What started with abundance may conclude in dismal
> 　　dearth.
> And it really will not matter then who started it or ran it
> If development results in an entirely plundered planet.

The Federal Government as an Inadvertent Advocate of Environmental Degradation

Charles R. Ross

Beyond any doubt our environment has seriously deteriorated. Accepting this fact, we must determine how and why this happened and then, hopefully, suggest what we can do about it.

Those of us who have had the privilege of serving in the federal government must bear a good portion of the responsibility for the current sorry state of environmental affairs. In a popular phrase of the day, most of us had "tunnel vision."

How could such a thing possibly happen? It certainly was not because your government official or employee deliberately set out to ruin the nation. A review of the Department of Interior's Conservation Yearbook Number 4 for fiscal year 1967 shows that there were people in government who could talk the proper language. The Department expresses great concern for "Man . . . an Endangered Species" in the yearbook which, for the most part quotes the right persons, such as Kenneth E. Boulding, René Dubos, Robert Oppenheimer, and others. Former Interior Secretary Steward L. Udall himself says: "We need a man-centered science which will seek to determine the interrelationships of life, interrelationships whose understanding will enhance the condition of man."

President Johnson, in Executive Order 11278 establishing the President's Council on Recreation and Natural Beauty on May 4, 1966, declared, "To be isolated from that natural America is to

Charles R. Ross, a lawyer by profession, was chairman of the Public Service Commission in his native Vermont when he resigned in 1961 to accept an appointment by President Kennedy to the Federal Power Commission. He was renamed to the FPC by President Johnson in 1965 and resigned in 1968. He has been one of three U.S. members on the International Joint Commission, and now is a consultant in the utility field and for the New England Regional Commission.

be impoverished—no matter how different one may be. To destroy it, to treat it carelessly, is to disregard one of the profound needs of the human spirit."

Glenn T. Seaborg, Chairman of the Atomic Energy Commission, said on January 6 in the 1969 *New York Times National Economic Review*: "Many thoughtful people believe and fear that the technical civilization we have created is out of hand, that as a macro-system guided by large economic and social needs and forces, man as such is no longer in control." He suggested that our instinct for survival would carry us through, that we should not despair but must search in the deepest recesses of the human heart and conscience for the key to the future.

In the same issue of the *New York Times,* however, political scientist Zbigniew Brzezinski wondered whether our society would be able to survive the challenge posed by the technitronic society. He asserted: "On the contrary, the instantaneous electronic intermeshing of mankind will make for an intense confrontation straining social and international peace. *In the past differences were livable because of time and distance that separated them. Today, these differences are actually widening, while technitronics are eliminating the two insulants of time and distance.*"

As a former government official who has participated, I can assure you that men like Udall and Seaborg, Presidents Johnson and Kennedy, were and are sympathetic and understanding. However, as socioeconomist Robert Theobald has said, it no longer suffices for a person to have "meant well" if his intervention worsened rather than improved a situation. The right to interfere comes only through possession of information, knowledge, and wisdom.

What went wrong? Why is it we have such a faculty to ignore the wonderful speeches and reports that call our attention to the really pressing problems of the times? Way back in 1916, the National Academy of Sciences in its "Summary Report on Natural Resources" said: "Perhaps the most critical and most often ignored resource is man's total environment. . . . The effects on man himself of the changes he has wrought in the balance of great natural forces and in the new microenvironment which he has created are but simply perceived and not at all well understood."

It would appear that these remarks must have had some impact in government, judging from the quotations by Udall, Seaborg, and Johnson. Yet, the Ford Foundation is willing to spend a goodly sum of money, along with Yale, to talk some more. Let us hope that there will be action as a result of these series of lectures.

Any action, of necessity, must be directed at the very institutions that sought and have been charged with the responsibility of enhancing and preserving the quality of our environment. Government, industry, and the university have let us down, and have left it up to tax-exempt foundations to carry the ball. It is really tragic that this great nation of ours has to rely upon foundations to provide the funds to those who are concerned and, in a few cases, to those who want to do something more than research or study the problem. Unfortunately, most paths lead to just a few foundations.

The relationships of industry and the university with government, in effect, have actually determined the inadvertency of the environmental degradation. In order to put together the complicated, long-range plans for tomorrow, an almost incestuous relationship between these unholy partners has developed, and such "minor" problems as the environment have been lost in the shuffle. Surely, few can be really surprised by my statement that our institutions have let us down. John Gardner, [former] Secretary of Health, Education, and Welfare, has worried about it; economist J. Kenneth Galbraith has talked about it at length. Yale Law Professor Charles A. Reich has focused on the helplessness of the individual citizen in confrontation with government and business. Andrei D. Sakharov, the Russian nuclear physicist, has written eloquently about it. In an essay which appeared in the *New York Times* on July 22, 1968, he wrote: "The division of mankind threatens it with destruction. Civilization is imperiled by: a universal thermonuclear war, catastrophic hunger for most of mankind, stupefaction from the narcotic of mass culture and bureaucratic dogmatism, a spreading of mass myths that put entire peoples and continents under the power of cruel and treacherous demagogues, and destruction or degeneration from the unforeseeable consequences of swift changes in the conditions of life on our planet."

This is what I am really saying: the environmental degradation suffered by our nation has been inadvertent in the sense that our institutions have become one critical mass. The checks and balances which each institution provides for the others are no longer as effective. "I am earth's nature: no rearranging it," said Robert Browning. The unholy three, in their eagerness to rearrange nature, have failed to appreciate the dangers to the environment. However, if it is entirely inadvertent, there is hope because we may be able to do something about it.

I have spent ten years of my life in regulation of industry. During that time, I have had the pleasure of participating in the great American game of awarding certificates to the lucky holder of the right combination of experience, money, and political pressure or pull. I regret to say that regulation—one of government's technological arms, the so-called fourth branch—is as guilty as the legislative or executive branches of government in failing to understand the consequences of its decisions. These awards, which Professor Reich has discussed, are not made entirely on merit. They reflect the human characteristic of a decision-maker who understands power and mistrusts new ideas and concepts, as well as the biases of the particular agency and the deterioration of governmental process.

Let me try to substantiate the viewpoint that government agencies can be very unresponsive to new ideas, but respond much more easily to biases of the "in group," the establishment for a particular agency.

Early in my career in Washington, I had several memorable experiences with the Department of Interior. The first involved an Arizona Power Authority application to build a large hydro-electric facility in the lower Colorado River, a project known then as Marble Canyon. The case is particularly interesting because it, together with the High Mountain Sheep and the Storm King cases, illustrates the schizophrenic position in which the

Department usually finds itself—a department dedicated to promoting pollution control, oil, gas and coal power, fish and national parks. It also portrays the righteous and indignant regulator who has a lot to learn.

The Marble Canyon project was expected to be the "cash register" for development of the Southwest by the Interior Department. It would provide the Department's dam builders with a beautiful project, large and massive. It would satisfy those who felt that Arizona and New Mexico deserved a better fate than Mother Nature had decreed. It would also show the Park Service who was boss.

However, the waters were muddied by the application of the Arizona Power Authority. The Arizona Power Authority was, according to some, a pseudo-public power organization fronting for the private power interests who were not about to let Marble Canyon be developed by the government. Poor California was present, gasping for its mammoth project and determined not to let its mortal enemies in Arizona win the sweepstakes. Poor Secretary Udall did not know what to do at first. Clearly, the conservationists were concerned, but the Interior Department would not support them. Finally, after the Examiner had issued a decision, the Department sought to intervene for the purpose of seeking federal development.

To make a long story short, we had oral argument; purely by chance, the conservationists were the beneficiaries rather than the victims. California and Arizona were so interested in dueling that finally Congress took hold and ordered the Federal Power Commission to slow down. Since there was a precedent in the case of the Grand Canyon from President Herbert Hoover's days, Congress was not as reluctant to step in as it often is.

Actually, the public versus private power issue became embroiled; Southern California Edison, seeking to prevent either Bridge Canyon or Marble Canyon, proposed another solution obviating the necessity of a dam on the lower Colorado. The proposal involved the construction of very large coal-generating stations in the desert. This is now underway. Knowing of the concern expressed by the Sierra Club and others, Udall has tried to make sure there would be as little impact on the environment, and especially on the Indians, as possible.

The Marble Canyon case illustrates the fairly typical bureaucratic response of someone who is challenged by an interested group seeking to present a viewpoint for which there are no supporting standard cost-benefit ratios or economic standards. The mammoth bureaucracy creaked into action. The Secretary of the Treasury issued an order to challenge the right of the impertinent conservation group, the Sierrra Club (a latecomer), to dare to go to Congress to try to prevent a power development. Much to the Sierra Club's ultimate benefit, it has tentatively lost its right to claim a charitable exemption. Now the nation has a group interested in the environment which does not have to play pat-a-cake with fund sponsors. There are already too many worthwhile organizations controlling purse strings which must apologetically decline to finance action groups seeking to advance similar causes— often the reason for their very existence. Boldness is not typical of many conservation organizations and officials. Plenty of learned talk, yes; action, no. Recognizing the hand that feeds you is just as typical of man as of any other animal.

I am reminded of a day in the closing moments of the Marble Canyon controversy, when the time was running out on the congressional moratorium for the Federal Power Commission. A sincere and dedicated woman from a well-known conservation group—not the Sierra Club—was sent down by some administrative assistant on Capitol Hill to see me. She was amazed to find out that the Federal Power Commission could possibly undo all that had been accomplished. Her organization had not really focused on the FPC as one of those terrible government bodies which are the curse of society. Today, I am pleased to say, the FPC is getting its fair share of attention, although it is not very easy to follow the activities of such an agency from afar, as I personally have discovered.

While the results flowing from the Marble Canyon controversy are not as unfortunate as they might have been, most individuals would agree that it turned out as well as it did through no fault of the government. In this case, inadvertency worked to the public's benefit.

The High Mountain Sheep case is another classic conservation case. A group of private utilities proposed a power dam to be located on the Snake River, somewhat above the confluence of the Snake and the Salmon rivers, on the Idaho-Oregon border. A competing group of public power agencies proposed a much larger alternative project which would dam up both rivers. Here, the initial issue was essentially public versus private power, with federal power standing in the wings.

The principal antagonists decided early in the game that conservation, "fish," would be a factor. The private power advocates were well aware of the muscle that the fish people could exert. In fact, it has been alleged frequently that the private groups have used the fish people to kill public power projects. The public agencies decided to go whole hog and urged the largest possible projects with an attitude of "Damn the fish; full speed ahead." The Commission, with me writing the decision, elected to support the small project because it felt strongly that it was very important not to dam up the Salmon River. By this time the public power group had gotten the message that we might do this; as an alternative, it suggested that it could be talked into building the smaller project. The Feds (Interior Department) were sent into action during the closing moments of the game to pull the fat from the fire for the public bloc. They succeeded. I can still remember Justice Thurgood Marshall—then Solicitor General—arguing forcefully to Chairman Lee C. White and me that the government should take the necessary legal steps which might lead to a really large public power development, irrespective of fish.

Once again, those interested in safeguarding our environment are the inadvertent beneficiaries of governmental indecision. It now turns out that the Interior Department can prove from a fish standpoint that the High Mountain Sheep site would be prejudicial to the fish runs up the Salmon, even though it was not physically blocked. So they now want to build at another site farther upstream. The time that was bought inadvertently by the government and power interests enabled Congress to look again at the value of the Salmon River for purposes other than power, and it gave Justice William O. Douglas a chance to sound another clarion call to his nature-loving brethren. Frankly, I would not bet on any dam on the Snake. The environment-minded ladies in tennis shoes, meanwhile, are learning what it takes to survive in the cruel world of politics, where man eats man and not even gracefully at that.

These two cases, as well as the Storm King case, are really the exceptions that prove the rule. It scares me to think that the results were achieved almost by chance. I told a group of economists at the Institute of Public Utilities at Michigan State University: "You must do your job well as the guardians of our economic system. This means you may have to get your feet wet; you in turn may be accused in indignant tones of being a politician or you might even lose some good consulting jobs or the prestige of government contracts or employment. It could even involve your university in the messy but necessary life on the outside and serve as a constraint in attracting capital for the next year's building program. This is your choice. I know I got sick and tired of regulating by the seat of my pants, and it wasn't because I didn't try. Give my successors something better. But don't expect a performance under regulation better than what the so-called 'real world' can do."

The academic community concerned with the environment has a duty to see to it that the decision-maker, politician though he may be, is educated and that these decisions are not left to chance. Maybe it will not get all the glory, but its children will reap the benefits.

Now look at the other side of the coin, when society was not so fortunate. In 1912 the International Joint Commission (IJC), of which I am presently a member, was asked to explore the problems of water pollution from Lake of the Woods to the St. John River in New Brunswick, Canada. Some people may think the Department of the Interior just recently discovered that Lake Erie was a mess. It may surprise them to learn that back in 1918 the Commission officially warned the government that the situation in parts of the Great Lakes was "generally chaotic, everywhere perilous, and in some cases disgraceful." Some 51 years later, the two nations are told once again that the situation is serious. In fact, Lake Erie is said to be dead. Maybe, just maybe, this time, when the IJC comes out with its latest report on the conditions of the Great Lakes, the two governments will respond and not allow another 50 years to pass without significant corrective action.

I must mention the role of the Army Corps of Engineers. The Great Lakes provide the Corps with wonderful opportunities. Many states are bounded by the Lakes. This means many politicians. Many politicians mean many possible projects, which are proof of the individual politician's ability not only to survive in that Washington jungle, but to bring home the bacon. Just think of the harbors to be built and dredged, for example, and all the spoil that one has to get rid of. The Great Lakes "just by being there" are a challenge to any good civil engineer and politician.

For example, the IJC has a proposal before it to determine whether it is feasible to control the level of the Great Lakes. It also is supervising the dewatering of Niagara Falls; after all, we cannot let honeymooners spend the rest of their lives bemoaning the fact that the crest of the American falls is no longer the same and that those terrible boulders at the bottom destroy the spectacular effect. Furthermore, we cannot afford to let the Canadian falls be more spectacular than the American.

By the time of the origin of the Niagara Falls dewatering plan, the Commission was "on to" ecology, so we requested the Corps of Engineers to retain an ecologist to make studies of the falls before the project's start. He has assured the Commission that there is no reason to worry about an irremediable harm done by this temporary dewatering. The Commission takes pride, too, in the fact that it has managed to attach two outstanding landscape architects to its advisory boards. Hopefully, it is not too late to go back and crank into the Levels Study an ecological appraisal of such an effort. The thing that bothers me is that the happenstance leading to retention of an ecologist should not be dependent upon coincidences: a certain commissioner with an interest in the environment, or the rekindling of such interest by former Yale Law School student Frances Enseki, who belonged to what I used to call the Washington Conservation Underground—a group of young, knowledgeable, somewhat anti-establishment, diverse individuals, the real doers.

These young students and graduates, professionals if you will, actually more than anything else, give me confidence that the system can be licked. They have infiltrated all the government agencies, and tried out most of the nonprofit ones as well.

I had great pleasure recently in warning the FPC's Electric Advisory Council (one of those formidable combinations of government and business in which the consumer, the conservationist, or the man in the street is on the outside looking in). The FPC and its stepchild, the Advisory Council, were carefully discussing the future of the United States: where all the capital should be spent, and the argument of nuclear fuel versus fossil fuel. It was scarcely a simple exercise, since the power industry is the largest in the nation in terms of capital investment. Moreover, the subject dealt with energy. The Advisory Council was the same group which declined to look into air pollution a year or so earlier, jointly with the FPC. Such a subject, according to the Council, while important, was not really as necessary as discussion of how many nuclear plants could be built. Of course, the FPC could proceed on its own in such a study.

In any event, everyone understood everyone else's problem. Possibly, just to liven things up a bit and since everyone knew I was leaving the FPC, I thought I would try to leave them something to think about. There had been a lot of crying about the nasty people who did not understand the real values of life, such as cheap electricity. There were even people who insisted that power lines should be buried and some who questioned the Atomic Energy Commission about the dangers of radioactive waste, both in its discharge and disposal! Even more frustrating were those who were beginning to make a case about thermal "enrichment." Some more people were even trying to force the AEC with legislation to consider environmental factors!

The opportunity was too good to pass up. Briefly, I suggested to my fellow commissioners and the industry that the confrontation was not between them and a group of ladies in tennis shoes. Such struggles had been, and would continue to be, pretty unequal—even though individuals like Professor Frank J. Tysen of the University of Southern California, at the Thorne Ecological Institute in 1967 in Aspen, were urging these nice ladies to act like guerrillas. The new struggle would be between the establishment, in this case the FPC and the power industry (not such an unusual partnership as it seems at first glance), and the youth of today.

The young people would be armed with facts and spurred on by knowledge, not just emotion. They would be motivated by the thought that everything could end pretty quickly if too many mistakes are made. Unlike the older generations typified by those sitting in that meeting room who only have a relatively few years to live out, these youths have ahead of them most of a lifetime. Unlike us, they cannot afford the luxury of a mistake. Time has escalated, and the future becomes the present to them. "After us, the deluge" may be the motto of the industry but it is not theirs.

So I warned the industry that a revised power survey must deal with the environment, not just with natural beauty. I told them to learn something from the Bureau of Public Roads, that it would be their turn to be "on stage" during the 1970s and they should attempt to understand the ecological approach even if they did not agree with it. If they did not, I said, the youth of today would exact a stiff price, possibly going beyond dollars and cents. Their beloved institution, a semipublic business, might be forced, hopefully, to account for its mistakes.

Why such a warning should be necessary is not too hard to understand. In describing my FPC experiences to the Western States Water and Power Conference recently, I said: "It is too easy to become wrapped up in our own little world. We are too much aware only of industry and its officials. We know the latest political gossip in Washington. We are concerned about the impact of our decisions on those we happen to know. We try to be concerned about the impact of the decisions on the people we don't know, but it is difficult."

It is terribly difficult to be tough when it is necessary, if you are dealing with someone you know and like. The occasional visit to your office to say hello is a great antidote for a case of strict regulatory enforcement. As would any doctor, you pay more attention to those who complain than to those who do not complain but place their trust in you. It is good salesmanship to convince your regulator that only the two of you are capable of handling such technical and difficult problems.

To add to the soft sell, if it becomes necessary industry can turn to its true friends, those representatives or senators who understand the role of government and business. For the hard sell, discreet phone calls from distinguished senators from the "oil patch" or the current impoverished area as to the status of a particular case usually are informative enough for a good political regulator or administrator to get the message. Or possibly someone in the government needs more money which can be obtained from bonuses for offshore oil and gas concessions. There is even the possibility that upon leaving government you can secure a good consulting contract for your new firm with either industry or the local, state, or federal agencies—if you are a good boy. It is tempting. The loner who can resist the temptation finds life more satisfying but far more difficult.

Is it any wonder that to some officials and businessmen the environment or the quality of life for the average citizen is a relatively inconsequential matter when compared to the economic health of the industry?

As an example, the paper industry has successfully fought off attempts to clean up lakes and streams. In November 1963 I told the Inland Empire Waterways Association—a potent lobby for the Corps of Engineers: "To those who have been crying aloud, 'Let's clean up our streams,' I add, 'Amen.' To those who are polluting our streams, I say, 'Watch out.'"

This warning stemmed from my experience on the IJC, since for years the Commission had tried to secure some semblance of cooperation in cleaning up the Rainy and the St. Croix rivers, a fact that does not speak well for either industry or government. Here again, it is understandable; the government (in this case, local and state) was seeking to preserve jobs, and industry was trying to meet southern competition. Almost without exception, the members of industry argued that they would be forced to move to other communities which understood their problems better if pollution controls were enforced. The situation finally convinced even the most die-hard friend of the industry that the boom must be lowered on the states, even though federal-state relationships might suffer in the process. This meant taking the drastic step of removing the problem of water pollution from the Department of Health, Education, and Welfare and giving it to the Interior Department.

The solution, long in coming, was a political one which should not be forgotten. Too often the delicate ecological balance between the creature, the federal government, and its kindred creature, state government, is protected at the expense of the public.

Competition in providing citizens with the best government possible is not necessarily unfair. It should even be encouraged. In fact, we might get a government which recognizes that a place must be reserved within the decisional process for the expression of independent viewpoints by private organizations or individuals, although the average administrator or regulator does not like to be bothered by them. As a result of my experience in the Storm King case, I said in a speech to the Federal Bar Association in October 1967 that "No really satisfactory method has yet been found within the bureaucratic structure to give such expression to 'the full faith and credit' needed to expose each course of action to the fullest consideration necessary to reach the best decision."

In conclusion I said: "The commissioners for their part will have to recognize that a greater number of appliances which provide increased leisure will be useless if there is such disharmony between man and his environment that man is unable to understand himself and his relationship to the universe."

The real action should be in local or state government, and it ought to be able to improve upon the performance of federal agencies.

I guess it is obvious that I am somewhat critical of government and its innate ability to frustrate the average man in the street, although I still think public service is the most challenging activity available to man. The real gap is the credibility gap between the youth of today and their government, although the universities—the father but not the master of the technological man—are also wanting. I said in a letter to the *New York Times* in which I was proposing an environmental institute that "An environmental institute would also re-focus the energies of the universities from the defense establishment into avenues more consistent with the concerns of their students and faculties. There would be an opportunity for students, professors, and scholars in general to apply their knowledge to real problems—something they often need to feel the relevance of their scholarship—and to help shape the environment for the years ahead.

"An environmental institute, funded by grants from Congress, private industry, foundations, and other private and public organizations, may not solve all our environmental problems but it might be a big step in that direction. Isn't it worth finding out?"

In discussing new institutions to serve the individual, William R. Ewald, Jr., observes in *Environment and Policy: The Next Fifty Years:* "University people, as individuals, may create a stir from time to time about the future, but few communicate this and their institutions have somehow avoided learning how to do research on the future of the human species and environment, much less to teach it. The ring of truth is much louder and easier to follow in the hard sciences, where it is also more easily coupled with technology to find its way into the marketplace or weaponry and is more easily financed."[1]

This brings me to the methods and means which I feel can make our government more effective.

First of all, as case studies for future students, such an institute would be wise to follow a course similar to that which former Secretary of the Interior Udall suggested for Vietnam: make a behind-the-scenes study of the pressures, the influences and

[1] William R. Ewald, Jr., ed., *Environment and Policy: The Next Fifty Years,* (Bloomington, Indiana University Press, 1968).

factors which determined some of the important environmental issues of the day.

For example, what are the whole stories on Storm King, High Mountain Sheep, Marble Canyon, the Hudson River Highway, desalinization plants, the alleged deal between the Interior Department and Corps of Engineers on the estuary study or the language concerning offshore oil and gas development in the "Marine Resources Report," the Santa Barbara incident, the slowness of the nation to focus on strip mining, the inability or delay by both industry and the scientific community to grasp the significance of thermal pollution, the failure to consider esthetics until forced to do so, and the story of the alleged threatened Udall resignation under President Johnson?

We should examine the role of federal advisory committees and should research in depth the role of the foundations in the environmental field. I recognize and pay my respects to Laurance S. Rockefeller for his service to the nation in the field of environmental study, but I wonder why it should be necessary for everyone interested in conservation to go, hat in hand, to the Fords or Rockefellers for seed money. The federal government is found wanting, possibly because it is disinclined to finance some group which would cause it trouble by raising questions about the impact of federal actions on the environment. Of course, if one has sufficient independent resources, it is a different story.

I wonder, too, whether serious thought has been given to the makeup of advisory committees. Is the public completely represented, or did we have chiefly people from Texas in the mid '60s, people from California or the West in the late '60s? Or are these committees composed of respectable, rich public members who know and understand each other?

We must analyze the role of the conservation organization, from the elite Audubon Society to the rip-roaring, gun-toting hunting clubs. Somewhere there should be an institution which the citizen can trust for sound scientific and social judgments on environmental issues. We have enough guerrillas. We need a Peace Corps type of Institute for the Environment, not a think tank for waging bigger and better wars. I could suggest men for 50 institutes tomorrow if they could be established, and the war in Vietnam would not even miss them. The world, however, might profit from their efforts.

It is hard to establish the need for a new institution because, of necessity, you are forced to expose the weaknesses of the old. This leaves you subject to the charge of being either an anarchist, a revolutionary, or just a frustrated old man. It helps when others have similar thoughts and your brilliant concept is not unique, although it may have been original with you. It is encouraging, too, to discover that others are also determined to prevent a multiplicity of organizations from cashing in on the ecological rage.

Through the generosity of Thomas Watson, Jr., who made one of his employees, William Ross (no relation), available, and with the cooperation and assistance of former Vermont Governor Philip H. Hoff, a Vermont Institute for the Environment is under consideration. Some might accuse us of merely seeking to emulate the university. I do not think so—at least not the type of university we know today. We would intentionally structure our institute to promote and even possibly force interdisciplinary consideration of environmental problems. We would attempt to remove the threat of domination by any single vested interest or any one individual. Like the Peace Corps, we would program a continuing renewal of personnel and the replacement of any individual after a proper period of time.

In general, we want to restore the faith and confidence of the people in the environmental decision and give them a role in shaping it. This means the youth of today, who will have to live with the mistakes of today—if the mistakes permit survival. This credibility will stem from youth's confidence in the independence of the participants, a confidence that the university sought to achieve in asking for tenure.

Last and most important, the institute would be *action oriented.* It would even include politicians! It might just get the job done if it could get off the ground. More work is required on our part, of course, but it is hard to shake the world and still earn a living, just from a time standpoint alone.

Originally, I had hopes for a national institute. A recent colloquium at Washington soon convinced me that the conservation establishment and Congress were not ready, so I lowered my sights to Vermont. Now, New Hampshire (Dartmouth University) is interested, as well as Massachusetts (Williams College). This is familiar territory—at least Vermont—and offers promise. What pleases me even more is that there seems to be a provincial northeast underground. I am exchanging ideas, including possible new legislation, with New Hampshire through a fascinating group of people who have similar opinions. I am also serving as an adviser (unpaid at my request, in order to preserve my objectivity and freedom from conflict-of-interest charges) to the Lake Champlain Committee, and through them I keep in touch with others, particularly in New York State.

We are making progress. The adversary process, the Victor Yannacones[2] and the courts are, of course, helpful. "Knowledge power," in the words of Ewald, is even more effective. Lawyers, and I confess to be one, are not known for their innovative contributions. They are essentially conservative and serve as a brake for most of society, at least for those who respect the past and are intimidated by a lawyer's ability to express himself.

Loyalty to institutions, religious or otherwise, for loyalty's sake is a luxury this universe can no longer afford. We must challenge our institutions and our dogmas. Maybe, if we even challenge industry's or government's right to do as it sees fit, unless proved by others to be damaging, we would be better off.

We should require those who propose new technological advances to assume the burden of investigating and reporting the potential impact of such developments on society. Possibly, if this were to be done, the federal government would not be the inadvertent advocate of environmental degradation.

I can see progress.

[2] Victor Yannacone, a New York attorney, organized the Environmental Defense Fund in 1967 to create a new body of law by litigation on behalf of all U.S. citizens.